CH00728448

SURROGATE MOTHER

SURROGATE MOTHER

One Woman's Story

Kirsty Stevens with Emma Dally

CENTURY PUBLISHING
LONDON

Copyright © Kirsty Stevens 1985

All rights reserved

First published in Great Britain in 1985
by Century Publishing Co. Ltd,
Portland House,
12-13 Greek Street, London W1V 5LE

British Library Cataloguing in Publication Data

Stevens, Kirsty
   Surrogate mother : one woman's story.
   I. Title   II. Dally, Emma
   306.8'745   HQ759.5

ISBN 0 7126 0783 8

Printed in Great Britain in 1985 by
Anchor Brendon Ltd, Tiptree, Essex

Contents

CHAPTER ONE

Making the Decision

WHEN I WAS a little girl I dreamt about having a great adventure. Sometimes the adventure involved magical creatures and enchanted forests; other times it would be knights-in-armour. When I grew up I did have a sort of adventure – an experience unlike any other and completely unpredictable. But it had nothing to do with fairies or forests or knights-in-armour.

The adventure began one evening in 1982, when I saw a television programme about surrogate mothering in America. I had never heard of the subject before, so I watched with interest.

I learned from the programme that a surrogate mother is a woman who has a baby for an infertile woman unable to have one herself. The sperm comes from the husband of the infertile woman and is implanted in the surrogate mother either by artificial insemination or through sexual intercourse. When the baby is born, the surrogate mother hands it over to the natural father and his wife, who then adopt it as their own.

I watched the programme with mixed feelings. As a mother of two young boys, I could sympathise with women who were unable to have children. I felt terribly sorry for all these infertile women. It seemed so unfair that some people had more children than they wanted when others couldn't have any at all. Thousands of abortions were performed each year to end unwanted pregnancies while hundreds of couples would do anything to have a baby of their own.

Surrogate mothering seemed to me a perfectly acceptable way of dealing with the problem. I didn't see anything morally wrong in the idea of one woman finding another woman to have her husband's baby for her. After all, plenty of women have babies by artificial insemination with sperm given by anonymous donors, yet no fuss is made about them. And, as someone who loved being pregnant, I could understand how fertile women would be willing to have a baby for someone else.

What bothered me about the programme were the surrogate mothers themselves. The women interviewed all seemed to be doing it just for the money. They saw their bearing a child for an infertile couple as a business like any other, with leases and sales and contracts. Except that here, the lease was on a woman's womb, and the product being sold was a baby. There was no contact between the surrogate mother and the adopting mother, no emotion involved, no sense of the great importance of the creation of a new human life. And these arrangements, like all business transactions, attracted the usual extras – agents and lawyers all getting in on the act for their own gain. I thought that was tacky and seedy. Here were these unhappy women willing to do anything to have the child that their own bodies were denying them, and they were surrounded by people whose only interest was in making money. I regarded the whole subject with deep reservations.

After that programme, I started noticing other signs of interest in surrogate mothering. Stories on the subject appeared in the press, and on television and the radio. My initial objections changed little: everyone seemed to be in it for the money – everyone, that is, except those poor women who couldn't have their own babies.

Then I saw one article that really changed the way I

thought about surrogate mothering. This was about a woman who had acted as a surrogate mother for her infertile sister. There had been no money involved, and no agents or lawyers or contracts. This baby had been born for love, not for financial gain, and it suggested to me that surrogate mothering didn't have to be a seedy business. It was possible, after all, for one woman to bear a child for another as a loving gesture. That I approved of.

After reading the article, I started thinking more about the whole idea. And I wondered whether this might be something I could do myself. The idea grew slowly, and I found myself thinking about it seriously.

I thought about it, first of all, because I did have the ability to have babies. It was something that came easily to me. Both of the times I got pregnant it happened when I wanted it to, and both my pregnancies had been uncomplicated. Since I had this ability, why not use it to help others? Why not bring some happiness to a childless couple, a couple who had no hope of having their own baby? I had seen on television and in the articles I read that childlessness could be an incredibly destructive force in people's lives, with their overwhelming desire for a baby practically taking them over and destroying all other joy in their lives. Seen from this point of view, surrogate mothering was a kind and generous act; and the story about the sisters proved that it could also be a warm, emotional experience. More and more I realised that the idea of doing this had become something very attractive to me. It was no longer just a thought, it was a definite desire.

Having a baby for someone else is the ultimate gift of love. When the woman had a baby for her sister, the emotional bond between them must have been stronger than ever as a result. I realised that if I ever did this, if I had a baby for another woman, the emotional closeness would have to be the most important aspect of the deed. I would need to get close to the people I had the baby for, so that in the end I would be giving them their baby as a gesture of friendship.

3

In the light of what happened, I can now see that my insistence on this may have been naive. Nonetheless, it was the most crucial element for me from the very beginning of my involvement with surrogate motherhood.

*   *   *

My wanting this kind of closeness must have come from something more fundamental than a simple desire to help others. These were reasons that had a lot to do with the current state of my marriage and my life generally, but they went back ultimately to my childhood and the way I was brought up myself.

I was not getting along all that well with my husband. John and I had been married for five years, and we had two boys, aged three and four. For some time I had been feeling that John did not act as responsibly towards us – as a husband and a father – as I thought he should. I was always the one in charge of running the house, looking after the children and generally keeping everything going. I also had a clerical job in an insurance company which brought in money that we needed to live on. John is a very talented commercial artist with a good job, but I thought he lacked ambition. And during that time he was acting as if he were still a bachelor. I felt that we had drifted apart and that, in many ways, there was little contact between us.

We rarely argued about these problems because, although I am forthright and say what I think, John tends to be retiring. He avoids serious problems whenever possible instead of facing up to them. He can't stand conflict, and lets me have my way if opposing me means making a fuss. My life with him was rather dull and unsatisfying. At the time, I didn't feel that our relationship could really give me what I wanted.

Nor was motherhood alone supplying the interest that it once had. I love my sons very much but, by 1982, as they reached an age at which their dependency on me was steadily lessening, looking after them was getting to be less than a full-time job. And my clerical job brought in money but it was not very demanding.

I suppose that other women reach this sort of impasse and start to wonder whether there's anything left for them in life, anything more on the horizon. Some probably start to think about finding some form of excitement outside their marriage, such as other men. I was in a similar position, but that wasn't my way of dealing with the problem. I'm just not that type. I am an adventurer by nature, but not in that way. I love my family life, and still felt committed to my husband, even if we were going through a rocky stage in our marriage. I had no intention of breaking up our home (or anyone else's, for that matter).

For one thing, I was extremely proud of my lifestyle. We were in the process of buying a house; my children were good boys, bright and healthy and nice little people; and, between us, John and I were beginning to earn enough to afford many luxuries that I would never have dreamt of owning when I was younger. We had a car, a freezer, even a video recorder (which the boys did their best to monopolise). To me, this had a lot of the elements of the good life about it.

If that sounds materialistic, I am not ashamed to be considered as such. I like having material comforts around me, and trying to surround myself with the physical signs of financial security is an important part of my personal happiness.

I think that anyone who has had an upbringing like mine would feel the same way. My mother was an alcoholic, a bad alcoholic; she had been that way for as long as I could remember. My father walked out on her when I was nine and my sister Mary was four. I hated him for deserting us all. It was only later that I realised that my mother's drinking must have driven him away, though I'm still not ready to forgive him. When he walked out, he walked out on us too.

With father gone and my mother as good as gone, I had to take on most of the responsibility for the home. My mother was completely indifferent to the squalor she created around her, so I was the one who tried to keep Mary and myself clean, scrubbing the few clothes we had every night in the hope that they would be dry enough to wear to school the next morning.

As for a relationship with my mother, there basically wasn't any. She had terrible moods, black and angry and wild, when you couldn't even talk to her. I became very accomplished at avoiding her when she was like that, but sometimes it wasn't possible, and then she would lash out at me or Mary with whatever she had to hand. Many times she swung at me with a broken bottle, though usually she used her fists.

At school I learned to keep up a façade. I knew that all the other girls had nice mums, whom they talked about and did things with like shopping, and how I envied them! But I never let on about my own.

When I was twelve, my mother remarried. She met a man (in a pub, naturally) who was several years younger and on the rebound from a recent break-up. He was attracted to her bubbly personality and didn't realise what he was letting himself in for.

This second marriage changed her for a while. She drank less and pulled herself together, and she became nicer to me. My step-dad was nice too. He worked as a van driver for a big haulage company and he liked Mary and me. He treated us gently and with real friendliness, and sometimes bought us treats and presents as if we were his own kids. Even when he and mother had their own baby, a wonderful little boy they called George, he treated us like his own. For a short time I had a normal home life, like the girls at school.

It didn't last. My mother went back to her old ways shortly after she had George, which was when they had been married about a year. Within months she had slipped into her old ways again and, when George was about three months old, my step-dad walked out. He had been driven away just like my own dad, unable to take any more of mother's wild behaviour.

This time my mother was worse than ever. She drank more, made worse messes and was really violent when she got hold of Mary or me. Worst of all, she was completely incapable of looking after the new baby.

I had to be George's mother. I fed him and changed him, dropped him off at a day nursery on my way to school and picked him up on my way home. I took him for his check-ups at the clinic and no one ever asked any questions. Maybe they thought he was my baby.

When George was six months old, my mother disappeared. One day when we got home from school she wasn't there, and she didn't show up again for three months. She had done this several times before, just left like that without a word, but never for that long. This time when she returned, it was too late.

While she was gone, I tried to make it appear that our lives were normal, never letting on that anything unusual had happened and hiding my mother's disappearance from anyone outside. Not that many people seemed to care. I forged my mother's signature to collect her social security payments each week and we managed to live on that. This was not easy. My mother was a smoker, and she used to buy her cigarettes 'on tick' at the local shop, paying off her bill when she collected her social security. I continued buying them 'for mum' even while she was away, fearful that the shopkeeper would get suspicious. I couldn't take the risk, but I used to wonder sometimes if there was any way to trade the cigarettes for food at another shop.

I kept this up for about two months, and in a way I quite enjoyed it. We had a better life than when my mother was around, at any rate. The flat was clean and tidy, and so were we; there was no threat of violence, no more filth, no bottles

7

by the sofa. George went to the nursery, and Mary and I went to school. Behind the pretence, we were relatively settled and normal.

It couldn't last. One evening the doorbell rang and I went to open the door. There were two women social workers and two policemen standing there. The social workers looked me up and down, then looked behind me into the flat. One of them spoke to me in a cajoling voice.

'Hello dear, is your mother at home?'

George was sitting in his rocker nearby and I grabbed him fast. I knew what they were up to.

'No,' I said to her. 'She's out. She'll be back soon.'

'You don't know where she is, do you?' She spoke in that same cajoling voice.

'No, she went out and didn't tell us.'

They all stepped inside, still friendly and smiling, and persuaded Mary to come over to them. I backed away, still holding on to the baby. One of the policemen tried to snatch him, so I screamed as loud as I could. George started to scream too. Every time one of them came near me I screamed again, and George joined in. After a minute they realised I wasn't going to give up that baby without a fight.

In the end they sat it out, just plopped themselves down and waited for me to give up or fall asleep. The hours rolled by, and I sat there wide-eyed, glaring at them all.

Finally, at 4 a.m., I couldn't keep my eyes open any longer. I fell asleep, and they grabbed George from my arms.

After that we were all taken into care and separated. I never forgave the social workers for taking George away. A few months later I was allowed to see him once. He didn't recognise me and seemed quite happy where he was. That hurt me more than anything else in the world. To this day I don't know where he is, or even if he's still alive.

*   *   *

I was sent to live with foster parents in south London. I didn't like them one bit. The woman was a complete cow to me, and had only taken me in to make money as far as I could tell. I tried several times to complain about her to the social services but they ignored me. I was only fourteen; how could I possibly know whether they were suitable foster parents? It was during that dreadful time that I realised something important; if I was going to get anything I wanted, I'd have to do it myself. Nobody was ever going to help me. Since that time I've had quite a lot of happiness, and have known people who are good and kind. But I've had to do most of what I've done on my own. I may have been a fourteen-year-old kid, but I was right about that.

When I was sixteen, I discovered boys and started drinking. It was boyfriends who bought me the drinks. I felt good being out with them, but I also felt nervous, and thought that drinking would make me feel a part of things, like a real grown-up.

Most of the time I drank gin and bitter lemon: gin because I thought it was sophisticated, bitter lemon because it hid the taste of the gin! I used to knock them back one after another and soon I got a reputation for it. 'Kirsty can drink *ten* gins in one go,' people used to whisper about me. I never got drunk, just merry and wild. I'd do crazy things like jumping on the bonnet of a double-decker bus and offer a bag of chips to the driver, then jump back off when he started moving. They were all silly things like that, but I thought they made me smart.

One day it struck me how stupid I was being. I was drinking more and it was costing more – the friends weren't always there to pay – and I was intelligent enough to see where I was headed.

'I'll end up like mother,' I said to myself. That thought disgusted me so much that it made me stop drinking, and since then I have hardly drunk anything alcoholic. It's all cokes and orange juice for me.

My mother did turn up again, when we had all gone to our foster homes, but she made no effort to get us back. I didn't care. She had no right to call herself a mother. She had given us no care, no security, no love. The only emotions she seemed to experience herself were self-pity and violent rage, and I didn't want to have anything to do with her.

One thing I did get from her was a very strong idea of what a proper mother should be. I learned it the hard way, but I learned it well. Now, when people talk about the sacred mother-child relationship and how children should be raised by the woman who gave birth to them, I just laugh. It's not who gives birth to you that's important but who loves you and cares for you.

*　　*　　*

I met John when I was seventeen. He was an art student and I was working at Tescos, and we struck up a conversation when he asked me some question or other. Within a year we were married and two months later I became pregnant, as we had planned.

John comes from a good family, supported by all the security of home life and devoted parents. We lived near them for a long time and saw each other a lot, and that was great for me, especially when my first child was born. John and I got on very well, and I loved being a mother.

But life was not easy. John was adamant about not wanting me to work, so we were very poor. We lived in two shabby rooms and I was at home day in, day out, with the baby. As much as I loved him, this life wasn't enough for me. I felt stuck. And, not surprisingly, I got depressed – quite severely depressed. For a very brief time I saw a doctor about it. I was still depressed when my second son was born, and I didn't know how I was going to manage.

When the younger boy was a year old, I took matters into my own hands. I announced to John that I was going to take a secretarial course and get a job. I told him that I *had* to get out of the house, and that was that. By this time John was less inclined to oppose the idea of my working: he had realised how expensive children are, and he was barely earning enough to keep us fed and clothed. I did the course and got myself a decent job, and in no time my depressions were a thing of the past. I don't get them any more, and I saw that I could never allow myself to get trapped like that again.

I'd beaten my depression, but other problems began to arise. John tends to get fads, becoming wildly interested in some new hobby and spending all his time and money on it for months on end. He'd get interested in, say, motorbikes, and I wouldn't see much of him except at mealtimes. Sometimes I joked with him that I had been just another of his fads, and that he had got tired of me pretty quickly. I laughed when I said it, but deep down I felt that there was some truth in it. I was still very young and felt that I could and should be in control of my life. I had energy and enthusiasm and ideas for doing things. By 1982, when we had been married for five years, I was ready for something new.

I didn't talk to John about surrogate mothering for a long time. I held it back from him partly because we weren't very close, and partly because it was still only a fantasy.

As the weeks passed, however, I found that I was thinking about the idea much more seriously. It sounds like boasting to say this, I suppose, but I did think that I was perfect for the 'job'. I already had all the children my husband and I wanted, and, at that point anyway, I couldn't imagine wanting any more. But my body was still working well: it had proved itself fully capable of producing healthy babies without any trouble. I loved being pregnant and, at twenty-three, I was still very young. It seemed a waste not to take advantage of my child-bearing abilities.

Even as I mulled over the idea, I didn't want to talk to anyone about it. I realised straightaway that if I were going

11

to go ahead with the plan I would have to do it in complete secrecy, so it would be foolish to tip off anyone about my intentions by showing even the slightest interest in the subject. Doing it on my own would be difficult, but not impossible. I have a habit of running things through my own mind before attempting them, and in my fantasies I was already working out all the tiny details.

*　　*　　*

I began to wonder about the next step; finding an infertile couple who wanted me. I knew that in America all sorts of agencies had been set up to get the two sides together, but there didn't seem to be any in England. More to the point, that was exactly the sort of arrangement I was trying to avoid: agencies, lawyers, contracts, etc. I had to find the couple by myself, because only in that way would there be any hope of a friendly relationship rather than a purely business arrangement. No third party could help me with that aspect of it.

I realised even then that I was unusual in one respect: most surrogate mothers don't go looking for an infertile couple. Usually it is the other way around. My reversing the process might make me look very strange to some people, but there was no way round that. It was a chance I had to take. But where would I find them?

By a funny coincidence, it was a woman at work who came up with the answer. In passing she happened to mention that she had heard a radio programme about surrogate mothers, and they had talked about two magazines that might take small ads for infertile couples and surrogate mothers. One of these was a high-class magazine aimed at genteel readers; the other was a contact magazine.

This really excited me, and I resolved at once to put an advertisement in the high-class magazine. I knew that it was very respectable and I thought I might meet the right sort of people through it – people who had the money to give the child a good home.

I rang them and asked if they would accept an advertisement for surrogate mothering, and they said that they would. I wrote it that night and sent it off with a cheque. Two days later the magazine returned both cheque and copy. They had decided that they couldn't accept the advertisement after all because, they said, they didn't have a category to put it under. I suspect that they had taken legal advice and decided they shouldn't get involved. I was very disappointed, but there was nothing I could do about it.

So my only hope, after all, was the contact magazine. I sent in the same advertisement a few days later. It read:

SURROGATE MOTHER WISHES TO MEET CHILDLESS
COUPLE. DISCRETION EXPECTED AND ASSURED.

I had a box number because I wasn't going to be so stupid as to put my name and address in an ad like that. I hoped that an infertile couple might have heard the same radio programme my colleague had heard, and that they would be watching out for an advertisement by a surrogate mother.

The only thing to do now was wait.

Another possibility had also opened up. Confused by the whole issue and desperate to talk to someone about it, I had finally confided in a close friend of mine. She was surprised at first, and a little bit shocked; but, after the shock had worn off, she became very enthusiastic – almost as enthusiastic as I was. Carol knew me so well, and knew the ins and outs of my relationship with John, and she was sure that what I was doing was perfectly reasonable. Even when I had doubts about it, she convinced me I was being silly, and her certainty convinced me even more that it was what I wanted.

It was through Carol that I came across my first childless couple. They were business friends of friends of her husband, Americans who had been trying for years to have a baby of their own and had finally given up. Now they were looking for a surrogate mother to have one for them. Sharon asked if I was interested, and I said I was, at least in principle. After making discreet enquiries, she gave me their address, and I wrote them a letter.

This couple was very wealthy, so they satisfied the basic requirement of being able to provide well for a baby. But in other ways they were not so satisfactory.

First, they already had an adopted child and had decided they wanted to have one of their own. This didn't really fit in with my expectations, since I wanted to give the joy of parenthood to people who would never have it otherwise. I knew from my own childhood that just being the biological parent of a child doesn't mean that you love it any better, and, by the same token, there was no reason why they shouldn't get the full pleasure of parenthood from an adopted child. Second, they were both in their late forties. That meant that they would be in their late sixties before the child was considered an adult, and I didn't like the idea of that too much. I had no objection to older parents but if I was to choose I wanted people closest to my ideal.

Third, and foremost in my thinking, was that with these people all the way across the ocean, I would never be able to have the kind of close, emotionally charged relationship I was looking for in surrogate motherhood. And that was the most important thing for me. Perhaps it meant so much to me because I wanted to make up for something lacking in my own marriage, but for whatever reasons it was essential. These Americans were twice my age, and whatever contact we might have would come mostly from overseas telephone calls. Between those two problems, I knew that a relationship would have been impossible.

I was also alarmed by the speed with which they started talking about lawyers and contracts. From their very first phone call, in response to my letter, they were turning the whole thing into just the sort of business deal that I was trying to avoid.

14

But they were very keen to go ahead with it. In no time at all they had made me a very generous offer of over £25,000. This was too large for me to take seriously at first, truly a staggering amount. But, instead of wanting to grab it immediately, I felt under pressure from the American couple. I felt that they were trying to rush my decision by making me an offer I couldn't refuse. I sent them a letter explaining how I felt, but their reply hardly paid attention to what I'd said. They went to great lengths to persuade me. I wrote back again saying firmly that I hadn't made a decision and needed to wait a while. I wanted to see if there were any replies to my ad first.

It was at this point that I told John how deadly serious I was about being a surrogate mother. It did not come as a complete surprise to him, because I had mentioned the subject quite a lot. I can't say that he was overjoyed at the idea, but he didn't try to change my mind. He knows very well that once I've made up my mind about something, there's no stopping me. He is very much the passive partner in our relationship.

A few days after the issue of the magazine came out, replies started coming in.

Some were sad, some abusive, some ridiculous. One was from a homosexual couple who had decided that their little family could do with an extra addition. I didn't have to think very hard about rejecting them. Homosexuality doesn't bother me, but I do believe that the ideal situation for bringing up a child is with a heterosexual couple.

The majority of the replies, however, were from ordinary heterosexual couples. Most already had children, and the woman had been sterilised but later decided that she wanted to have another baby after all. Having discovered that the operation wasn't reversible, they wanted to get someone else to bear the child for them. Or they had remarried since being sterilised and wanted to have a baby that was their husband's, if not their own. Obviously these women did not qualify either, because all of them had children.

Only one letter, from a couple in south London, seemed to come from the sort of people I was looking for. I liked the sound of them straightaway. They had put their name and address on the letter, for one thing, which suggested that they were serious, open and honest people. They gave the full story of their efforts to have a baby: the wife's infertility, all the tests and operations she had gone through to conceive. It turned out that there was no hope: she had blocked Fallopian tubes and none of the operations had succeeded in unblocking them long enough for conception to occur. The doctors had advised her to try for a test-tube baby, but the success rate of this technique was too low – only a one-in-ten chance of the implanted embryo surviving and being born at term. In other words, nine out of ten implantations abort. Each try, each implantation, would cost about £3,000 whether it worked or not, and the couple felt that they simply could not take this expensive route when the chances of failure – and disappointment – were so high. The wife had been through too much already. They had also failed in their efforts to adopt either in Britain or abroad, so that avenue was closed off too. This was not through any fault of theirs. The man was past the age at which people may adopt children in Great Britain.

The woman was in her mid-thirties and the man was nearly forty. This was the second marriage for both of them. Her first marriage had broken down because of her infertility, and now they were having problems because she still could not accept her failure to conceive. They were desperate, they said. I was their last hope.

They signed themselves Robert and Jean.

I was nearly crying by the time I finished reading their letter. This couple had such a sad story, my heart went out to them. They were exactly the sort of people I thought I might be looking for.

I knew that I would get in touch with them before too long.

CHAPTER TWO

Our First Meeting

FOUR DAYS AFTER getting the letter, I rang the telephone
number given in the top corner of the notepaper. It was early
afternoon. The boys were still at school and the house was
quiet.

The phone rang five times before it was picked up. A
woman answered. Her voice was well-spoken and soft.

'Hello?'

'Hello,' I said. 'My name is Kirsty. I'm the lady who put in
the advert about surrogate mothering.'

There was a pause.

'Oh . . .'

Another pause.

'You know,' I said, 'the advert.'

'Oh, um, yes.' She obviously didn't know what to say.

I just waited and hung on because I decided she must have
been flabbergasted actually to hear from me. When she spoke
again, there was a little more decisiveness in her voice.

'It's lovely to hear from you. We're glad you called.' Then
she paused again, waiting to hear what else I had to say.

'The thing is,' I went on, 'I'm talking to other people as
well at the moment, and some Americans in particular, but
I've rung you because I would also like to meet you. I liked
your letter and I thought there wouldn't be any harm in our
meeting.'

'Oh, yes.' She sounded nervous but pleased. 'Okay. Would you like to come out to our house, or is there another place where you'd like to meet?'

'Your house would be fine,' I said, and asked when. We arranged for me to go round the following Wednesday at 8 p.m., and she told me how to get there.

'You'll both be there, will you?'

'Oh yes,' she replied. 'My husband will be here too.'

We said goodbye and hung up.

They lived in a south London suburb, so I had to take the tube and then a train to get to their house. I did feel a little bit nervous on the train, and suddenly had horrible thoughts about the couple I was setting off to meet. Would he be fat? bald? pimply? Would she be the same? Would they have peculiar habits and mannerisms? Going by their letter they seemed very nice, but you can never tell what somebody's like unless you've actually met them.

I wasn't so afraid of what they would think of me. I was ready to make a big effort to give them a good impression of myself, had put on a new skirt and a pretty blouse and cardigan and done my make-up especially carefully. I wondered how much I was going to have to do to convince them to trust me, to persuade them I wasn't out to con them. I suppose that if I were in their position, I'd feel more than a little bit suspicious of someone like me.

They lived quite close to the train station, and I was easily on time. Turning into their road, I saw that it was a tree-lined avenue of modern houses with decent-sized gardens – a nice, ordinary, quiet street. I said to myself, 'Well, they certainly live in a good area.' Already I was 'sizing them up' as prospective parents.

When I reached their house, I stopped by the gate for a moment. The downstairs lights were all on but the curtains were drawn, so I couldn't see anything inside. The porch light was on and a red car parked in the driveway. I did feel distinctly nervous now and I caught my breath. Reminding myself that I was in control here, I walked up the drive to the front door and rang the bell.

It was a man who answered the door. I was immediately and pleasantly surprised. He was tall and slim and relatively good-looking, with lots of thick black hair. He was dressed trendily without it being overdone – smart but casual – and he had a nice face with blue eyes and a strong mouth. He was definitely not my idea of a thirty-eight-year-old executive. He looked more the type to be a DJ, or something like that.

He stood in the doorway and stared at me. As far as I could tell, he seemed a little bewildered. Probably he was dumbfounded to see such a young woman standing there, to see that I was reasonably attractive and normal-looking. This seemed to take him aback, and he stared for the longest time.

'Hello,' I finally said. 'I'm Kirsty. The lady who put in the advert.'

He nodded and said, 'Oh yes,' as if he didn't know what to do. So I stepped into the hallway and held out my hand.

'How do you do?' I asked.

He smiled and shook my hand and then suddenly he seemed to come to life.

'How do you do?' he said. 'My name is Robert. Thank you for coming.'

Shutting the door behind me, he took me down quite a long corridor.

'My wife is rather nervous about the meeting,' he said. He had a deep voice.

'Oh yes,' I replied. 'I understand.'

He didn't say anything more, but led me to a room which I thought immediately must be their formal sitting-room – definitely not their den. There was a big wood fireplace in one wall with a coal fire. Everything was very dark and formal-looking – the wood panelling on the walls, the leather sofas, the beautiful wood coffee table in the middle of the room. They had expensive but very good taste.

19

I sat down on one sofa and he sat down on the other, opposite me. He took a chocolate from a silver tray on the coffee table and began to munch it, then offered me one. He had an attractive smile.

'No, thank you,' I said. I thought it was a funny thing to do, and wondered where his wife was.

At that moment she came in. She looked much younger than her mid-thirties – more like twenty-five or twenty-six, I thought at first. She had long, strawberry-blonde hair, a roundish face and wide-set eyes; she was slim and very pretty overall. She looked like the sort of person I'd want to be friends with, and I thought that was a good sign. She did seem nervous, however, so I smiled at her, trying to put her at her ease.

'I'm Kirsty,' I said. 'We spoke on the phone.'

'Yes,' she said quietly. 'My name is Jean.' She didn't shake hands and didn't say anything more, just sat down on the sofa next to Robert. When he asked if I'd like a cup of coffee and I said yes, Jean got up and hurried out to make it.

When Jean had left the room, Robert again told me how nervous she was. 'So we must be careful about what we say,' he added. I didn't know what to make of that, really. What was it that I was supposed to say? What did he want me *not* to say? I hadn't a clue.

Jean came back and handed me a cup of coffee, and then sat down. I don't know which of us was the most embarrassed. And there we were, three strangers looking at each other without knowing what to say. We were there under strange circumstances. I knew something that was very personal to them, that they dearly wanted a baby and hadn't had any hope of getting one. And they were sitting there facing a person who might possibly give them their hearts' desire. We all felt very exposed, and it was a strange feeling for everyone. I just sipped my coffee and tried to smile.

Gradually we began to talk. I told them that I wanted to

have a baby for someone else because I could, and I enjoyed it, and since other people wanted what I could do, why not? I added that there were other things I wanted out of the experience, and told them about the crucial emotional aspects that I was interested in. I wanted to be friends with them, I said, at least while this was going on – that it was important to me to have a close relationship with the people that I was going to do this most intimate thing for. I wanted them to share the pregnancy and birth through me.

I also explained that they mustn't raise their hopes, since I was still talking to another couple, these Americans, and hadn't made up my mind about them yet.

While I talked they sat close together on the sofa. At first they were both very quiet, letting me do all the talking. It was I who raised all the questions and problems, and when they didn't speak I answered all my own questions as best I could.

At first they listened and seemed happy with what I was saying, asking only the odd question. Jean continued to be very silent, so Robert did all the talking, but then she started talking too. All she said was that they wanted a baby; that was the only thing that mattered to them. She said that a few times, and after the first time I noticed that Robert nudged her to be quiet.

After a while, Robert started to ask me questions. He was very interested in the Americans, and kept asking about them. I told him I wasn't very stuck on them but we were still negotiating.

'Well, what's the fee?' Robert asked.

I wasn't prepared for this, to be talking about money on the first meeting. He probably assumed that money was the only reason I was doing it – in spite of what I had been saying – and he was very businesslike.

'I can't really say about the money yet,' I replied. 'I haven't thought about it enough. I have an idea about what I'm supposed to ask, but I'd rather not be pressured into talking about it right now. It embarrasses me to do that, and besides, that's not what I want out of it.'

Robert obviously had the subject right at the top of his list – I suppose with good reason from his point of view, but it upset me. Every ten minutes or so he raised the subject again, asking how much I wanted. I kept saying that I didn't know and couldn't say, even when – if – we worked something out.

Finally he asked, 'Have these Americans made you an offer?'

I thought I had to talk straight then.

'Yes,' I replied.

'How much?'

Again I told him that the amount the Americans had offered was irrelevant, because what they had offered was way out of order: more than anyone should be expected to fork out, and more than anyone should expect to receive.

'They're very wealthy,' I told him. 'They can afford to pay just about anything.'

He kept pushing and pushing to get me to name the figure, and in the end I got so fed up that I told him.

'My husband and I have just bought a new house,' I said. 'That's a big expense for us, and the Americans know that. They have told me they would pay me what our house was worth, an amount big enough to pay off the mortgage. On top of that they'll pay all expenses – fares to America and the medical expenses of having the baby over there in a private clinic, and any other legal fees. Everything.'

What I didn't say to Robert was that this was one thing I hadn't liked about the Americans: they were suggesting a swap, a house for a baby, and I thought it was wrong to buy a baby like that. It was wrong morally and in every other way. I was concerned that the baby wouldn't have a good life in a home like that, for all their money. They seemed to be the sort of people who would make the child all the things you try to stop your own child from being. Children are selfish and materialistic naturally, and one of the things about

22

being a good parent – for me, anyway – is trying to teach the child not to be like that.

But the money they were offering had to be taken into account. With all the expenses, their offer would probably amount to around £60,000. It was a hell of a lot of money, and could have set me up for life.

I didn't let on about this to Robert and Jean because I didn't want them to get the wrong impression about me, but I did say enough for Robert to get an idea of the sort of money being talked about. He went pale as it sank in. Drawing himself up in his seat, he spoke sharply. 'That's far too much,' he said. 'I couldn't possibly come up with that kind of money, and even if I could I'm not sure I'd pay it.'

'That's exactly why I said there's no point in bringing up the subject,' I replied. 'You were the one who pressed me to say what the Americans were offering, even though I told you I considered it irrelevant. And now you're getting the jitters.' I wondered why he didn't realise that, if I were only interested in the money, I'd never have phoned at all.

I continued, 'What they're offering me has nothing to do with what I might ask somebody in England. For a start, I won't have to commute to America, and things will be a lot easier in England. There won't be any legal or medical bills to pay. Besides, Americans always offer a lot more, and what I would consider fair isn't anywhere near that sum.'

He seemed a little relieved when I had finished.

'Good,' he said. 'Because I simply couldn't pay that much.'

As I sat there, I took in my surroundings. Robert had told me he worked in the media, and he seemed to do pretty well out of it. Maybe they couldn't spend £60,000 to pay for a child, but they were well-heeled and I was certain they had the money to support one. I didn't see the rest of the house on that visit, but it was obvious that they had plenty of room.

Throughout our meeting, Jean just sat and stared at me. She had a desperate look about her, something that suggested she saw me as the last hope she had in the world of getting a child, and she didn't want to lose me. She seemed to be pleading silently.

I spent an hour and a half there on that first meeting. When I left at about 9.30 p.m., I told them I'd let them know what I'd decided. They both saw me to the door and were very very friendly.

'Well, we look forward to hearing from you,' Robert said.

'Yes, yes, let us know as soon as you can,' added Jean. 'Please let us know.'

As I sat on the train back to London, I felt very confused. One encouraging thing about Robert and Jean was that they seemed to approve of my ideas about surrogate mothering. Jean, in particular, seemed relieved at the way I thought about it: she gave me the impression that, having met a surrogate mother she approved of, she wanted to hold on to me at all costs. There was no way she was going to let go. Once she started talking her nerves made her talk too much, and she made it clear that she obviously wanted this more than anything in the whole world. Whenever I had cautioned them that nothing was settled, that I might not be back, she kept saying, 'That's okay, never mind. If you decide on the other couple, we'll just have to accept it. But . . .' As far as she was concerned, I *had* to stay.

On the minus side, Robert seemed much more business-minded, more calculating and suspicious. First of all, he had checked me out in a way to see that I wasn't some kind of pervert who was having a joke at their expense. Of course I was checking them out too, so that was fair enough. But his interest in the money angle upset me a lot. He asked *so* many times, 'How much money do you want?', even though I told him I hadn't thought about a figure.

Still, despite Robert's behaviour at that first meeting, he did seem to be a nice person and I had got the feeling that with him and Jean I would probably get the warmth and closeness that I wanted so dearly. Obviously they could not pay me so much, but I wouldn't expect it.

On the other hand, the Americans were offering me a very tempting chance to make a lot of money – with an expenses-paid holiday in America thrown in as well! I knew that this was probably a chance I'd never have again. But with them the whole business was everything I didn't want from being a surrogate mother: cold, calculating baby-selling, purely for money.

During that ride home my thoughts seesawed back and forth. One minute I was having beautiful thoughts about myself and Robert and Jean, and how happy I could make them. It was very martyrish if also selfish at the same time, and I felt full of warm feelings. The next minute I was a donkey with a carrot floating before my eyes. Money! Lots of money! I mean, not many people can turn down the kind of chance to make it in the kind of quantity that I was being offered. Would I join the crowd, or stick by my original dreams of putting the relationship before cash?

As the train pulled into Victoria Station, I shut my eyes and took a deep breath.

'Come on Kirsty,' I muttered to myself. 'Be decisive! This choice can't be all that hard to make.'

And in fact it wasn't. I had hardly opened my eyes before I knew what I was going to do. The whole point of this venture was the relationship I wanted to have with whomever I bore a child for. No relationship at all seemed possible with the Americans. With Robert and Jean there was that possibility. I had to go with them.

I felt bad for the Americans, but assuaged my guilt with the thought that if they had that much money to throw around they would end up getting a baby from somewhere else. I resolved to write to them that night telling them of my decision.

With Robert and Jean, I thought it might be sensible to wait a couple of days before telling them. Even though I really had made up my mind, I thought it better to mull it over rather than jumping right in with the news. I might have a change of heart, after all. And I didn't want them to think I had no other options.

CHAPTER THREE

Getting to Know Them

Two weeks after my first meeting with Robert and Jean, I rang them again. Robert answered, and I told him what I thought was the good news.

'Well, I've decided to go with you and Jean, if you are still interested.'

I was expecting him to be very excited, but he said, rather cautiously, 'Oh good.' And immediately he added, 'How much will it cost us?'

I still hadn't thought about how much to ask for. I felt that I couldn't do it for nothing, and Robert and Jean had to be willing to show their commitment and compensate me for loss of earnings when I stopped working, but it wouldn't be an enormous sum and, anyway, an exact figure hadn't occurred to me.

I replied that I didn't know yet. 'I'll have a think about it and let you know. In the meantime, don't you think we ought to get together and talk about this?'

Robert agreed, though he still sounded cautious.

'Yes, that's fine,' he said. 'But at this stage I think it would be better if just the two of us met, without Jean. Until we've sorted things out a bit more, anyway.' He didn't want Jean to be hurt if I did turn out to be a crank, or if we couldn't agree on the money, or if anything else went wrong. He thought the hurt to her would be minimised if we weren't already friendly. I agreed to this, because I had seen that she was a nervous and sensitive sort of person. I agreed to meet Robert for dinner in a week's time.

I spent that week trying to figure out how much money I should ask for. Doing this made me feel mercenary, and I had trouble with it. I talked to John about it a little. He took an interest in the problem, and he was very helpful.

'I can't ask what the Americans have offered' I told him, 'because it's so phenomenally high. But I have to ask for something that's fair to me. How can I work it out?' It wasn't easy.

The first thing I had to take into account is what I'd lose by giving up work. There was no way I was going to claim maternity benefits fraudulently, or benefits of any other kind for that matter. That would be wrong. The only way I could go through with this without arousing someone's suspicion was to leave work early in the pregnancy and not go back. That was all fine, but I wasn't about to let my family suffer, so the sum lost would have to be made up.

There were other aspects to take into account as well: things that were harder to put a price on, such as the physical and emotional cost of the whole thing. However friendly I became with Robert and Jean, there would probably be complications, emotional or otherwise.

To begin with, there was the problem of which method of conception we were going to use: whether artificial or natural, it would be complicated and difficult, at least for me. Then there were the usual problems of pregnancy: backache, morning sickness, all that type of thing, which can make you feel very out of sorts. Also, I am very sporty-minded – I enjoy shooting and skiing and ice-skating – and for months I wouldn't be able to do any of them. I mean, I could hardly go out on an ice rink six months pregnant and risk falling on my back with someone else's precious cargo inside me! So my sports were out, my hobbies.

The pregnancy would also be time-consuming. I'd be

spending part of my days making all the visits to the GP and antenatal clinics. I have a life of my own, and even with my own children I never exactly delighted in spending all this time, having blood drawn and all the rest of it.

Then there was the pain of childbirth itself. This is something you never forget once you've been through it, and even if the labour went easily it would still hurt. And if there were complications like splitting, which happened to me once, the pain and trouble would be worse still. After the birth I would have to get rid of the milk, which I usually produce in huge quantities. (I fed one of my children for eight months.) Then getting your body back into shape, sitting and doing boring exercises for weeks afterwards. These were all the gory, not very interesting aspects of childbirth that I would have to go through whether I was doing it for me or for someone else.

I also knew I'd be kidding myself if I denied that I would care about the baby I gave birth to. However much I said that I was doing it for someone else, that it was someone else's baby and not mine, there would still be some emotional attachment to the child. I would have to get over the trauma of giving it up, just as I would if a baby I wanted to keep was born dead. There was likely to be a period of mourning, and that too needed to be recognised in the money I got from Robert and Jean. And it was a good thing I prepared myself for this from the beginning, because giving up the baby was not an easy thing to do.

Finally, I had to deal with my family at a time when I would be going through a rough patch myself. They would be going through the hard time too, and the money I got would be for them as well as for me. It would be for everyone's benefit.

I'm not complaining about this, or saying I should have been paid just for doing what I wanted to do.

On the basis of these considerations I worked out a figure of £7,000. There was nothing scientific about it: a lot of things you just can't put a price on. I showed the figure to John, who thought about it and then said it was too low.

'For that kind of money,' he told me, 'you might as well do it for free.' So he worked out his own figure, and finally came up with £10,000, which I realised was much more realistic. I told him I thought his was better, and thanked him for helping me.

'Sure,' replied John. 'I guess it's a sort of contribution.'

Looking at the price he suggested, I said that I wondered if Robert and Jean would be able to afford it. 'You can't exactly go to your bank manager and borrow £10,000 to buy a baby,' I said.

'From what you've told me,' replied John, 'it sounds as if they might.' He clearly didn't sympathise much with Robert and Jean's financial position. We had just paid our gas bill and we would be having trouble getting through the rest of the month.

'I don't know – they may have the money all tied up, in their house or something. Anyway, I'll find out soon enough.'

And indeed I did. Three nights later, Robert and I had dinner together at a little restaurant in Soho. We had no sooner sat down at the table than he popped his favourite question.

'Have you decided on a price yet?'

I was expecting it, so I didn't get as irritated as I had before. And this time, finally, I was able to give him a figure. After explaining roughly how I'd arrived at the figure, I named it.

'And, of course, this is compensation rather than a fee,' I said. We all knew it might be against the law for me to receive money specifically for the adoption of my child.

Robert just nodded knowingly. He said he wasn't surprised by the figure, having expected something along those lines.

'Though obviously I hoped it would be less,' he added.

I didn't say anything to that. I couldn't, really, though I

hated the whole money side of it even more. In a perfect world I wouldn't be asking for anything; in a perfect world he and Jean wouldn't need me to be doing this for them. The world isn't perfect, so I had to be compensated, and I had tried to be fair. He didn't seem to think I was doing otherwise. But he let the subject drop right then, which relieved me. The rest of the evening we spent talking about new films, our work, things like that.

When I went home that evening I told John what had happened, and said that Robert had hoped the figure would be lower. He took a firm stand about this.

'You're not going any lower. It wouldn't be fair.'

I was relieved that he said so. The fact that he was taking an interest suggested that he wasn't totally opposed to my doing this strange thing, even if he didn't really like it.

Over the next few months Robert and I met every other week for lunch or dinner to work out the details. First we clarified the financial side. Robert asked how I wanted the money, up front or in instalments or halves or whatever. I said I didn't want it up front or even half up front because if I didn't get pregnant or some disaster happened I didn't want to have to go through the process of giving it back. I might already have spent some of it, and I would be embarrassed about the whole thing.

Instead, I said I wanted most of the money after the baby was living with them, and only a small portion when I got pregnant. I suggested 10 per cent to begin with, which I thought would show his commitment. But if anything went wrong halfway along, the 'deposit' would be forfeited for what I'd already been through. That seemed all right with Robert.

Then, I said, I'd like half the remainder two months after the baby was born – so they would have time to be together as a family without any financial pressures – and the final balance two months after that. Robert seemed quite happy with this. Although I knew that he and Jean weren't really short of money, I could also see that handing out large sums all at once would not be easy for them.

Once that was settled, we talked about the legal aspects of what we were doing. We knew that it wasn't illegal for me to be a surrogate mother, but at the same time we thought there might be legal traps we could fall into if we weren't careful, and obviously we wanted to avoid them.

For me, the big area of uncertainty was what right I would have to maternity benefits. I doubted that there were actually rules about this, but I knew that as a surrogate mother I couldn't go to a citizen's advice bureau and ask about them. I didn't think I would be entitled to the same benefits as a normal pregnant woman. Whatever the case, I knew that the best way to avoid any kind of fraudulent claim was to play it safe and not make any claim at all: no benefits or free dental care or anything else. By not making any claim I wouldn't be breaking any laws.

This also meant that I couldn't ask for any maternity pay, and I decided that I would give up my job at five months just to simplify matters there completely. I wouldn't be getting my employers involved in any way or acting fraudulently towards them. If I left soon enough, I wouldn't be entitled to maternity pay, and that would be that. I also decided not to go back to work for them afterwards, since that too would complicate matters by giving me rights I didn't want. If I did go back to work, it would be for another firm altogether. I could say that I had left my other job after becoming pregnant and hadn't planned to work again for a while, but that I had had a still-born child.

We both thought of going to a solicitor to have some kind of contract drawn up. But it didn't take long to realise that that was pointless: in English law a mother's rights over her child are absolute, so whatever happened I would have legal rights to the baby. If I decided to keep it after all, Robert would not be able to do a thing about it. A contract wouldn't be worth the paper it was written on. They could take me to court but I'd end up with the baby and they'd still be childless.

So the arrangements had to be based on trust. They had to believe that I'd give up the baby once it was born and sign the adoption papers when the time came. I had to trust them not to change their minds at the last minute, leaving me literally holding the baby, and that they would hand over the money as agreed. We discussed this at length, the need for trust, for a friendly relationship, how we could be friends. We also discussed whether we would try to be friends after the baby was born, but there was no answer for that. There wouldn't be until it actually happened. You can't know what you will want afterwards.

After two months of meeting each other every week or so, we had become quite friendly. We were able to laugh and joke and tease each other, be sarcastic in a friendly way without getting hurt or emotionally tripped up. And I felt that there could be some kind of relationship between us, over and above the arrangement about the baby. I thought that this might be something lasting, something permanent, though we both knew it was possible that the whole relationship could end immediately after the baby was born, to save any complications, any traumas. We just didn't know.

Robert said that he and Jean planned to tell the child about its conception and adoption whenever it was old enough. They would say that Jean wasn't its biological mother, that there was another woman. I would be described, said Robert, as 'somebody very special, someone to look up to and admire'. He would explain why I had done it for them, so that the child wouldn't feel rejected or dumped, and that everything was done out of love. He would say I'd helped them out of friendship and emotion, not as a business transaction. All the things that he was apparently going to say about me were pleasant, beautiful things, and I was very pleased when he told me about them.

33

I think there were things about me that pleased Robert, such as the fact that I wasn't going to press them for the final payment immediately the baby was born. It also pleased him that I didn't insist on having all the financial arrangements over and done with at the beginning, before I would allow myself to become pregnant.

Another thing that Robert liked was that I wanted them to be there at the birth if possible – to actually see the baby they would raise as it came into this world. For Jean, I thought, this was the next best thing to giving birth herself, a tremendous experience. For me, her being present was an important part of the whole idea of sharing the pregnancy, or as much of it as she could. I wanted her to know everything about the carrying of her child, without rubbing it in that she couldn't do the same thing herself.

They both seemed very happy at the idea of being present at the birth, but in other ways I thought Robert was being overly protective of Jean. He always stressed the importance of not upsetting her, which I understood, of course, but he was also too controlling, speaking for her all the time even when her views were different from his. We found this out when we had a little flare-up in a restaurant where we were having lunch.

Actually, I was the one who had the flare-up. I had said I wanted to talk to Jean about the pregnancy, to tell her when the baby was moving and all that sort of thing. And I wanted to talk about babies in general – to have girl-talk with her, separate from Robert. He said he didn't think she should know too much, that it might upset her to know all the details. Well, that did upset me: how was I to have a close relationship with *both* of them if Jean and I couldn't talk about these things?

I brooded about this for a long time, and then, one day over lunch, it all came out. I just blew up at him out of nowhere.

'You're being *much* too protective of Jean,' I told him. 'I can't speak to her, I only hear what she thinks through you, it's like the baby is all yours and she has nothing to do with it. Do you *really* know she doesn't want to hear anything about it, are you *sure* she doesn't want to talk to me?' I couldn't restrain my anger over this. We often bickered, but it was usually friendly bickering. This time I was really cross, and he knew it.

But it was a good thing I blew up at him, because he came to our next meeting all apologetic and sheepish.

'I got the wrong end of the stick,' he told me. 'I went home and talked to Jean about everything, and I see now that she really does want to know about this, she does want to be present at the birth, she does definitely want to talk to you about babies. I was wrong.'

This made me feel a lot better: I had felt I was losing my emotional grip on any relationship I might have with Jean, and that bothered me. The whole thing was threatening to be much more one-sided than I wanted it to be. But now things were sorted out and on a much more even keel. Robert and I went back to our friendly bickering and didn't get angry with each other for a while.

It's hard to explain, this friendly bickering. It was a personality clash, very basic: there was nothing personal in it. I did like Robert a lot. But both of us were the dominant partner in our own marriages – probably domineering too – and we were constantly trying to be the dominant one in this relationship as well. We spent hours trying to trip each other up, to get the upper hand. It never worked, of course. We were both too bloody-minded. It wasn't meant in a nasty way, even though we both got upset sometimes. I'd go away and brood about something Robert had said, and on our next meeting I'd come back and say, 'You said this and this, and that upset me,' and then we would work things out.

We had to remind each other when this happened what a strange position we were in. 'This is a bizarre situation,' Robert said one time, 'and there are bound to be times when the sheer tension of the whole thing makes us bug each

35

other.' This happened fairly frequently, I suppose: there were certainly occasions when I got absolutely furious with Robert, when he seemed to be thinking only about himself, his own problems. I'm sure he felt the same about me, but it never got out of hand. We were both so determined to get the upper hand, it was actually quite funny.

Robert's attitude was that without his sperm there would be nothing: no baby, no reason even to know each other. In his opinion, therefore, he was the star of the show. This feeling surfaced at one lunch when I had been saying how important it was that Jean be involved in the pregnancy.

'What about me?' he demanded suddenly. 'I'm part of this relationship, too; I play an important role. You seem to have this idea that you and Jean will toddle along sharing your pregnancy and leave me sitting at home alone. I don't want to just be forgotten about. You can't push me out in the way you're trying to do.'

I suppose this was similar to what a lot of men feel when they think about becoming fathers – that their woman is going to forget about them as soon as she's got a baby, and they'll be left out. None the less, I thought it was a silly thing to say and I over-reacted.

'Of course we know you're there, for God's sake!' I really snapped at him. 'We can hardly fail to notice it – you certainly remind me enough. But don't forget about me, either. I'm the one who is actually going to *have* this baby. I'm the one who'll look like a baby elephant for months, and have backache and everything else. Doesn't that count, or are your problems the only important ones?'

We both calmed down whenever we had got something like this out of our systems, and it was pretty quickly forgotten.

I couldn't let the tension out on my husband, either. Apart from taking an interest in the money he was pretty much indifferent to the whole thing, and I didn't really feel that I could talk to him about it. Nor at that point did I have anyone else to confide in: my friend Carol was off for a year in Germany, where her husband's firm had sent him.

I think that some of the conflicts between Robert and me came from our different backgrounds. My working-class family – very low down on the social scale – and mediocre home life, were worlds apart from Robert's professional middle-class existence. But even though we weren't social equals, we were equals when it came to basic cleverness. Robert knew this, and I think he resented it a little bit, so perhaps some of our friendly animosity came from that. And perhaps there was also an element of chauvinism. I did sometimes feel that Robert thought women were of a lower order than men.

Robert's social snobbery came out at one of our early dinners, after I had told him something about my background. He listened to my story and then offered to teach me a few things about etiquette! Being a nice, polite young lady, I just grinned at him sweetly.

'If you like,' I replied. I took no notice but thought he had been very rude, and I thought to myself, 'He ought to learn some manners himself before he goes teaching them to me.' But I didn't say anything.

I didn't even say anything when he told me, at that dinner, that he was a nice guy.

'I'm a nice person and people like me,' he said. Just like that, as if he were saying that he played tennis or liked sausages or something matter-of-fact. I'd never heard such a ridiculous thing before, and I could hardly believe he had really said it, but I sat there and smiled at him. He seemed to know that he had made himself look stupid, so he quickly changed the subject.

My lower-class background often makes me feel inferior or ill-at-ease with other people, and I always take casual comments to heart. Remarks that other people might ignore will hurt me deeply, and I brood about them for days afterwards. The person who made the remark would probably not be aware of having upset me, and I think that this often happened with Robert.

Our class differences also came out in the way Robert often teased me at restaurants. Whenever we went out, he would almost always have a bottle of wine and I would have an orange juice. I don't mind if other people drink, but I hardly ever do it myself.

Robert just couldn't understand this. Even though he knew about my mother being an alcoholic, he would make fun of me because I wouldn't have wine at meals. I got a definite impression that he wanted me to feel guilty about not joining in.

Another thing he laughed at was my taste in food. There are only certain things I eat – basically plain, simple dishes – and I like them cooked in a very specific way. So whenever we went out I ordered plain steak and chips or something else like that. I like my steak very well done, and I always said this in restaurants: 'burnt well done'. That's the way I like it.

Well, Robert thought that was hilarious. Orange juice and burnt steak! I might as well have asked for Fairy Liquid and an old shoe. As far as he was concerned, the only normal food was the sort he liked, things like chilli con carne with a huge baked potato and masses of sour cream. And he always had plenty to drink. He thought I was unsophisticated not to drink any wine, but I thought that he drank too much – a whole bottle by himself, usually, after having already drunk a lot at one of his business lunches. I thought I showed my own sort of sophistication by not drinking. But Robert had his own ideas.

It was annoying, the sort of bickering we sometimes got caught up in. And I did not like the way Robert often took the mickey. But we never talked about reconsidering the plan, never thought we might be doing the wrong thing. For both of us, I think, these little disagreements were mainly a way of releasing tension. In most ways we were very well-matched, Robert and I, and despite the occasional friction, I knew that he was basically a good person.

* * *

At the same time that I was working out the practical details with Robert, John and I had been talking about how we would deal with my family, and with the neighbours. I had thought a lot about this, and had decided that I didn't want anyone to know about it – not my friends, not John's family, not the neighbours. Some of the people I know can be very cruel and are capable of keeping a vendetta going against enemies for years, even bringing their children into it. I couldn't face such a thing happening over something which was nothing to do with them. I couldn't risk it: if they were too narrow-minded to understand, which I suspected they would be, it would be disastrous. I'd have to live with them, to face them every day. Even moving, if it came to that, couldn't remove the label they would permanently attach to me. So I had to keep it a secret.

What I couldn't keep secret, of course, was my shape. Sooner or later it would be obvious that I was pregnant. So I decided I would tell the neighbours when I was about five months. I would say it had been an accident, unplanned, but make it clear that I was going to carry it to term. Then, while I was at hospital, John would break the news to everyone that the baby had been stillborn – that it had a weak heart and couldn't survive the birth. And I was staying in hospital, so the story would go, due to depression and need for aftercare. He would say I was too upset to have any visitors, and eventually I would come home.

John and I both thought that this was the best way to do it. People would not ask many questions for fear of upsetting me, and would just stay away for a while 'until Kirsty gets over it'. Then they would come round and say how sorry they were, and before long everyone would forget about it. No complications. This seemed by far the easiest thing to do.

I asked Robert what he and Jean were going to say to their families and friends, and to my surprise he said they were going to tell them the whole story. Apparently Jean's mother knew that Jean had no hope of having a baby herself, and had already suggested that they find a surrogate mother. So they were going to be very open about the whole thing. Anyone who wasn't a close friend or family member would be told that the child had been adopted.

* * *

It was at about our sixth meeting that the question of conception came up. We obviously had to agree on what method to use, and nothing had been said about it.

It finally arose when all three of us went out to dinner together – only the second time that I saw Jean before I got pregnant. We spent nearly two hours making small talk: wasn't it a lovely day? don't they make unusual cocktails here? things like that. Anyone listening to us would have thought we were friends of another friend who had planned to be there but couldn't make it at the last minute.

I went off to the ladies room, and while I was there, it suddenly hit me that we had to talk about this. It had obviously hit them, too. No sooner had I sat back down than the conversation completely changed course.

'Now,' said Robert, 'what about conception?' Jean looked at me keenly as he spoke.

Although I thought it was natural to be talking about this, I got very embarrassed and went all red in the face. We had been talking about the weather a minute before and now we were talking about how Robert and I were going to conceive a child.

Robert and Jean were pretty cool about it, considering the circumstances. They were both smiling gently. I spluttered a little, and Robert helped me out.

'What I mean,' he said, 'is what method would you prefer?'

Those weren't words I was happy with, particularly the way they came out. Whichever way I answered, I was bound to feel funny about expressing a 'preference'. If I said that I wanted to do it the natural way, I might give the impression that I was dying to leap into bed with Robert. On the other hand, if I insisted that I wanted artificial insemination, I might appear to be saying, 'I don't want to get anywhere near you, thank you very much.'

As it happened, for a number of reasons I did prefer the natural method. My reasons were mainly practical ones. If we used AI, we would have to find a sympathetic doctor who was willing to do it, and that might be difficult – especially on the NHS. Going outside the NHS would mean more expense to them, and we had already agreed that we would make an effort to keep their costs down to a minimum. Also, before I could be artificially inseminated I would have to go through tests to make sure I couldn't conceive in the normal way. That would be messy and time-consuming, and being poked and prodded by the doctor would be extremely unpleasant and embarrassing. Besides, the tests were bound to show that I could conceive without AI, so the doctors would wonder what I was up to. I had heard of do-it-yourself AI kits but none of us had any idea of where to get one – except perhaps from your own GP, which we obviously could not do. So the natural method, though not really what I wanted, seemed the lesser of two evils.

But how to say this? After humming and hawing I finally took a deep breath and plunged in.

'Well,' I said, 'it isn't really a matter of preference, but I think the natural method would be best, or at least easier and cheaper...' I explained all my reasons.

To my astonishment, they agreed immediately. I was especially impressed by the speed with which Jean went along with the idea. I mean, she couldn't have been all that keen for her husband to be going to bed with another woman. On a moment's reflection, though, I realised that she knew we were not planning to do it out of some deep yearning for each other. It wasn't an affair we were having behind her back – we were going to bed to conceive a child for her, and for no other reason. So even if the idea made her uneasy, presumably she must have come to terms with that feeling. Also, she probably wanted to get it done as quickly as possible, and the natural method would suit that purpose much better than AI. So we were agreed. It had been easier than I expected.

It wasn't quite so easy telling John what we had decided. His face went white and he opened his mouth to protest until I explained all the reasons for deciding as we had. He didn't say a lot about it after that, and I think he understood that it was for the best. But I knew he wasn't pleased.

I also knew that agreeing on the method was much easier than actually putting the plan into action. As I lay in bed that night, I thought to myself, 'Well, this is where things start getting complicated.'

I had known that this would have to happen sometime, yet I couldn't quite convince myself that it was real. My feelings were a mixture of mild terror and total disbelief as I tried to make it sink in. But the more it sunk in, the faster my heart raced. I tried to think about something else and failed miserably. I had trouble getting to sleep that night.

CHAPTER FOUR

Becoming Pregnant

THE DECISION TO conceive naturally was made easier for me by my certainty that we would succeed straightaway. I reckoned it would only take a couple of tries, if that. I'd never had trouble conceiving before, so I was sure I wouldn't this time either. Little did I know.

The next step was deciding where to go, and this was a real problem. Love in the back of a car was out, for a start. I wasn't having any of that. And Robert annoyed me when we discussed the subject.

'Obviously we can't go to my house to do it,' he told me.

I was irritated. '*Obviously*,' I said. 'Give me a bit of credit – as if I'd want to do it at your house, with Jean there and everything.' I added, of course, that we were not going to go to my house for the same reason.

I said we could probably get hold of a friend's flat or house, but I didn't really like that idea. We would be surrounded by other people's property, their bed and their sheets and everything, and I didn't think I'd be happy about that. In the end we decided that the best, most neutral place would be a hotel. We both came out with the idea at the same time.

There was never any question of finding the most romantic hotel. Robert knew a place near his office that wasn't too expensive, and said he would book a room there when the time came. We had an unspoken agreement that he would pay. I said I would stay overnight because I would have to be still for a while after we had intercourse, and anyway I didn't want to have to travel at two o'clock in the morning. Robert agreed. He would stay overnight as well so that it would be easier for him to get to work.

'Are you going to tell Jean, or just say you're working late?' I asked. I wondered how she would feel about her husband going off to spend the night in a hotel with another woman.

They had worked this out already, and Jean didn't seem too troubled by it. Robert had said that if he didn't come home one night she wasn't to worry. She had smiled, knowing what he was talking about. That's what he did whenever he went to the hotel. He simply told her he wouldn't be home, or she would see him packing a bag and nothing needed to be said. I suppose she considered his 'infidelity' a small price to pay.

After all those years of trying to have a baby with Jean, Robert obviously knew all about menstrual cycles and so on, because he asked if I was going to take my temperature to see when the best time would be. I said that I probably would, and that when my fertile days came I'd phone him at work and say I'd see him the following day. Robert agreed.

Neither of us said so, but we knew that the next meeting would be at the hotel.

At this point I suppose I was actually quite excited to be putting our plan into action after such a long time. But I was also worried about being embarrassed when Robert and I went to bed together. I wasn't very experienced and I didn't know how to get through it – what to do, what to say, anything. After all, I was a virgin when I got married: I'd never been with any man except my husband.

Robert was much more experienced. He had been married once before he married Jean, and had obviously had relationships with other women, so I assumed it wouldn't be half as difficult for him as it would be for me. As things

44

turned out, he did have an easier time in some ways – but in other ways he was even more clueless than I was.

I was also quite worried about being away overnight as far as the neighbours were concerned. I occasionally went to stay with my sister, so I told John that if anybody asked where I was, he should tell them that. Since I'd be showing up at work with my overnight bag, I'd have to make up some explanation there too.

I did start to take my temperature but I found it difficult to read the thermometer accurately, so in the end I gave up and relied on my periods, which are always regular anyway. I knew that around the fourteenth day I was the most fertile, and that it was a good idea to have intercourse on the thirteenth day of my cycle.

I counted the days, and on the twelfth I rang Robert and told him I'd meet him at the hotel the next day after work. He hesitated for a moment, and I wondered if he was suddenly getting cold feet. But then he said that was fine, except that he had a lot of work to do and couldn't be there until 7.30 p.m.

That evening I told John that I was going to be away the next night. He just nodded, and then he said something I hadn't expected him to say.

'You won't let him do things to you that I do, will you?'

I was surprised. 'What do you mean?' I asked.

'You know, just what's necessary. Nothing more.'

I assured him that there would be nothing more and that he wasn't to worry. After all, I wasn't exactly looking forward to the experience myself. That was all John said. I was pleased that he had said it, and that he really didn't want anybody near me. But he understood that I had to go with Robert because it was necessary.

After work I went to the hotel. I left at about 5 p.m. and it took about forty-five minutes to get there, so I had about an hour and a half to kill. I had brought a book with me and sat in the hotel foyer and read for the whole time. I had told

Robert I didn't want to sign in, that I would wait till he arrived before going up to the room. I was perfectly happy to wait downstairs.

The only problem was, the chairs in the foyer weren't meant for lounging around in: they were very uncomfortable, and I began to get terrible backache. By the time Robert arrived I was in agony, and the pain continued for hours afterwards. At the time I thought it was rather funny that I was the one who had the bad back. But although I could see the humour in the situation, generally I was feeling very tense. The sight of Robert arriving made me more tense still.

Robert booked in and we got into the lift to go up to our room. I slunk in behind him, neither of us saying anything. The room was like any ordinary hotel room, two double beds, a chest-of-drawers and wardrobes all down one wall. There was a window, a television set and a private bathroom. The room was quite expensive, about £70. I was beginning to feel very embarrassed and I think Robert probably was as well. He started to unpack his bag and put a few of his things away – hanging up his jacket and so on. There was a little table with two chairs by the far wall. I headed straight for that, sat down and lit a cigarette. That made me feel better, and soon Robert relaxed a little too.

'Shouldn't you be asking me if I've had a nice day at the office, dear?' he said. I laughed.

'Well, did you?' I asked. We were joking around in our nervousness.

When he had put all his things away, Robert asked if I'd like to go and have dinner.

'I think we should have a drink first,' I replied. He laughed and said that was a good idea, he could do with one.

We went downstairs to the hotel bar, where I had an orange juice and he had a Scotch on the rocks. We chit-chatted over the drinks, about nothing really. Then we went to the dining-room to eat. I ordered my plain steak and chips and Robert kept taking the mickey out of my choice. He

46

ordered a bottle of red wine for himself – he knew full well I
didn't drink – and knocked the whole thing back. I could see
he was looking for a bit of Dutch courage, which was
understandable. Even with his greater experience of sex, he
obviously didn't find this any easier than I did. But I also
began to worry that he would get too drunk. He said he had
already been drinking at a business lunch, and I could see
that he was getting tired. His eyes were red and bloodshot.

Still, we carried on our jovial banter throughout the meal.
One of my interests is the occult and I mentioned this in
passing.

'Why are you interested in that?' asked Robert. 'Are you a
witch?'

I smiled. 'Maybe – you never know.'

'Are you going to put a spell on us tonight to make sure it
works?' he asked.

'You never know,' I repeated. 'We'll let nature take its
course, and then if it doesn't work I'll put a potion in your
tea.'

Robert laughed.

I was still very nervous, and Robert didn't make things any
easier by occasionally patting my knee in a friendly gesture.
This made me jump. I'm very funny about people touching
me, and I was increasingly anxious about what would
happen later, in our room.

We didn't finish our meal until around 11 p.m. Robert was
really quite tiddly by then – he had a brandy after dinner –
but we couldn't string it out any longer. We'd gone through
all the banter and we were both getting tired. It was the
middle of the week, and the only thing either of us really
wanted to do was to go to our own homes and get into our
own beds.

Leaving the restaurant, we sauntered through reception
and took the lift up to our room. My heart was racing. Robert
turned on the TV and disappeared into the bathroom, and
after a few minutes he came out wearing a blue dressing-

gown. I looked at him and my heart began racing even faster.

'I've been dreading this moment,' I said. I thought I might as well be honest. He smiled, saying nothing. I went into the bathroom and came out with a nightdress on. It was pink and knee-length. I had bought it the week before at Marks & Spencer. I stood there, not knowing how I was supposed to behave. Robert was already in bed, watching television, so I thought, right, this is it, and got in on the other side. I lay next to Robert but not close to him, making a funny sort of effort to keep my distance I suppose. I was still so nervous I don't know what I was thinking.

We lay like that for a few minutes, watching television and neither of us talking. Then Robert made his advances.

He began by putting his hand on my thigh, just lightly, not moving it very much. I leaned over and kissed him, and he seemed very surprised.

'I didn't think we were allowed to do that,' he said. I blushed, embarrassed.

'I don't know any other way,' I replied. My voice was hoarse and croaky.

Robert smiled. 'I'm not complaining,' he said. I wondered if perhaps I shouldn't have kissed him, but I didn't know what else to do. We just weren't getting anywhere, and I could only think about getting to sleep, I was so tired.

After a while I suggested that we sit up and watch a bit of television.

'Good idea,' said Robert. He sounded relieved, and I think he was happy I had made the suggestion. I asked him if he would like a drink out of the little mini-bar they had in the corridor. He said yes, so I popped on my dressing-gown, picked up some of his change from the dressing table and went down the corridor to the slot machine. I came back with a miniature bottle of brandy, which he drank in bed. It was close to midnight.

Eventually we both relaxed a little more. The brandy and the rest seemed to take the pressure off a little bit. Also, when

I got back into bed I lay right next to him, not away from him. He had his arm around me as we watched television, and we were close and touching without doing anything sexual. This helped us both calm down, and made things much easier.

After about half an hour I decided I'd better prod him into action, so I snuggled up a bit closer and pecked him on the cheek. It wasn't really a sexy sort of kiss, more a friendly one. But it seemed to be the right thing to do: this time he responded, and everything went fine from then on.

When we finished we were both so tired I knew we wouldn't have any trouble falling asleep. I got up to turn off the television and have a cigarette, and when I got back into bed we lay there in the dark talking. We didn't talk about anything in particular, and certainly not about what we had done. It was pretty strange, lying next to someone you've just had intercourse with but acting as if nothing had happened. But that's the way it was. When I heard Robert's breathing getting shallower, I stopped talking and allowed myself to drop off. When I heard him snoring I relaxed completely and fell asleep.

* * *

When I woke up the next morning it took me a minute to realise where I was. I had been a little nervous about the morning, and had wanted to wake up before Robert. That wasn't to be. Peeping over to find out if he was awake too, I saw that he had his eyes open.

'Good morning,' he said. 'Did you sleep all right?'

'Yes, thank you. Did you?'

When he said that he had, I replied that he must have done, because I could hear him snoring. We both laughed.

Robert started to get out of bed. I didn't take a look, obviously. He went into the bathroom to have his wash, and while he was in there I got up, put my robe on and smoked a

49

cigarette. When he came out of the bathroom I went in and got dressed. Robert had started packing his bag, and I sat down to put on my make-up. We didn't say much to each other.

We had decided to have breakfast together, and we went downstairs at the same time. Throughout breakfast we chatted about this and that, still not mentioning the night before. Then it was time for Robert to leave for work.

He apologised again for having to rush off, and I was still drinking my tea, so I finished my breakfast while he went to get his bags and pay the bill. He came over to the table and kissed me on the cheek.

'Bye, speak to you later.' Then he was gone.

Afterwards I went up to the room to collect my things, and went out to get the tube to work. All the way to the office I had my fingers crossed as I hoped my period wouldn't come that month.

* * *

That evening I made a special effort to be nice to John so that he didn't feel bad. I gave him a kiss and a cuddle, and told him, 'I missed you last night.'

'I missed you too,' he replied. 'Not being in bed with me.'

'Never mind,' I said, 'It won't be long now.'

I didn't say anything about Robert at all. I couldn't help feeling guilty and I didn't want John to feel left out.

I asked if anybody had asked where I was, and John said that one of the neighbours had come over and he'd told her I was staying at my sister's. So far everything seemed to be going all right.

Two weeks later, my period came. I was very disappointed, and John shared the feeling even though it was nothing to do with him, really. Robert took it surprisingly well when I phoned him to break the news.

'Never mind, we can't expect it to work the first time,' he

said reassuringly. He didn't seem bothered.

But I was. It wasn't just that I had thought I was so unfailingly fertile – even more than that I was disappointed because I didn't want to go through it all again. And the more nights I had to be away, the more difficult things were likely to get with the neighbours. That excuse about my being away at my sister's would start to look feeble (which indeed it probably did by the time I finally got pregnant).

*　　*　　*

The next month at the same time Robert and I went back to the hotel. Everything happened more or less exactly as it had done the first time, except that I decided not to wait in the foyer. I checked in myself and waited in the room instead.

Unfortunately, I signed my real name in the book by mistake. I didn't realise this until the next day. When the waiter arrived I signed the chit with my real name, then crossed it out immediately, pretending I had signed in the wrong place. The waiter assured me that I could sign anywhere on the chit so I did, using Robert's surname. But it was then that I realised I had also used my own name downstairs.

This alarmed me, but it was too late to change the signature. And when I told Robert about it later, he didn't seem too worried.

The evening before, as we were walking through reception to go up to our room after dinner, I thanked Robert for the meal.

'Shhh!' he whispered. 'We're supposed to be married! You don't thank your husband for dinner.'

I thought that was not very nice of him.

The sex was much easier this time. We didn't need two goes. I did try very hard to respond to Robert. It must have been hard for him to have sex with a woman while trying to touch her as little as possible. Neither of us felt that we were

51

committing adultery against our partners: this sex was embarrassing and difficult.

Afterwards we sat up and talked. This time we weren't so tired, so we put the telly on and I ordered tea and coffee from room service. We got out of bed to drink it, but eventually we got back in and drifted off to sleep.

My period came at the end of the month, and I felt terribly disappointed all over again. I was very depressed, knowing we'd have to go back to the hotel.

But that was nothing compared to my disappointment the third time my period came on. That time I got really angry, particularly as I was wearying of the one-upmanship and bickering that continued to flare up between Robert and me. That third month Robert had told me that he would be very late getting to the hotel from work, so we arranged to meet at the swimming pool next to the hotel.

When I go swimming I like to have fun, just paddling about and enjoying myself. When Robert arrived, he got into the water and started zooming up and down the length of the pool as if he were in training for the Olympics. He looked at me paddling about and a little smirk crept over his face as he trod water.

'You can't swim, can you?' It was less a question than a challenge.

'I most certainly can swim,' I replied indignantly.

'It doesn't look that way to me,' he said.

'Well, I came here to enjoy myself, not to compete in an Olympic marathon. If you want to show everyone what a good swimmer you are and get exhausted, feel free – but don't expect me to join you.'

He looked a bit put down, and floated off. I think he did feel a little silly, but I didn't like getting into those sort of arguments. It certainly didn't make anything easier between us for the rest of the evening.

My period came again, and I was really upset. It happened on a Saturday when I was walking down the high street with John and the children, doing the shopping. I had been talking to John about it, and told him I thought I was pregnant this time.

'I'm not absolutely sure like I was with our boys, but you never know,' I said.

Then, suddenly, there was blood gushing down my leg. My periods always start in a big gush like that, but this was the first time I'd ever been caught outdoors, unprepared. I thought, 'Oh Christ! I'd better get home quickly.'

I don't know why I hadn't been wearing anything. Probably it's because I hoped so much that my period wouldn't come. I always get terrible cramp and feel depressed for the first couple of days, and now all of that was much worse than normal.

Luckily, Robert and Jean didn't seem at all bothered even now. They had both been expecting it to take a little while. But I had no sympathy for that, and told them bitterly that I thought I'd be pregnant by this time. I was really beginning to feel that I had let them down after so much boasting about how I could get pregnant at the drop of a pin.

When my period came after our fourth try, I was feeling very despondent. I rang Robert and told him I was impatient, disappointed and worried.

'Well, we expected that it would take six months or so,' he told me. He said it kindly but he did also indicate, without really saying it in so many words, that he would start worrying if I hadn't conceived within another two or three months, but adding that there was no way he or Jean wanted to stop. They still believed it was going to work. They had a lot of faith, or maybe just a lot of hope. That was all for the better, because my own was beginning to run low.

It was after the fourth month that I realised my mistake. My younger son wasn't very well, so I took him to the doctor one day, and while I was there it occurred to me that I could get some free advice.

I casually said to the doctor, 'My husband and I are trying for another baby. Is there anything we can do to hurry it up a bit?'

The doctor was very pleased about this, being a Catholic. He showed me one of those temperature charts and started explaining it to me. When he said, 'You count the first day of your period as Day One,' I realised that I'd been making a mistake all that time. I'd been counting Day One as the first *after* my period had *ended*. I knew I would have to explain my mistake to Robert, and I felt like a complete fool. We would have to change the dates the next month.

I was embarrassed by my stupidity, but Robert was very nice about it, considering that he had been paying out all that money for the hotel and our dinners and everything on the wrong days.

This time I worked it out carefully and properly, and we met at the hotel again and had intercourse. As always, there was no loving in it, no deep affection involved, no feeling. There wasn't even any lust in it because we were always so awkward about the whole thing. We just had sexual intercourse in the most straightforward way possible, turned over on our backs and went to sleep, trying to forget that there was a strange person lying next to us in the bed.

Stupid things always went through my mind afterwards, as I'm sure they did in Robert's as well. For instance, I thought, 'I hope to God I don't snore all night and keep him awake!' And we often both lay there, fully awake, wishing to hell that the other one would go to sleep so we could be alone with our thoughts.

After that fifth try I hoped more desperately than ever that it was going to work. I knew I had done everything right this time, counting the days right and planning our intercourse for the best possible day. But still I was anxious, in spite of all my efforts to stay calm. I thought about all the reasons that my period was likely to come, to try and prepare myself for disappointment.

I had myself all set for it, and then, amazingly, my period didn't come when it should have done. As each day passed I got more and more excited, and I was amused that one of my first thoughts was, 'At last! I've done it! I won't have to meet him again at the hotel.'

But more important was the thought that it might have worked at last. 'Calm down, Kirsty,' I thought. 'You might just be late, the tension might be postponing it; your period might come any day.' I was almost lecturing myself.

John didn't say very much about it at all. I would tell him, 'Nothing's happened yet,' and he would reply: 'Good, good.' I would think, 'Is that all you've got to say?' I was very excited and, with my friend Carol abroad, there was no one I could talk to about the way I was feeling.

This went on for a whole week, and still my period hadn't started. I thought that now I could let Robert know, so I phoned him at his office.

'Nothing's happened yet,' I told him. 'My period hasn't come.'

His response disappointed me, just as John's had.

'Oh, yes. Well, we'll wait and see. We'll see how things go.' And I thought again, 'Is that all you've got to say?' But perhaps there were other people in the room and he couldn't talk. Still, I'd hoped for a little more enthusiasm.

Time went on. Another week passed. I decided that it was time to do a pregnancy test, so I bought one of those home tests.

The result was negative! I was so disappointed I can hardly describe how I felt. I thought, 'Oh no, I've imagined the whole thing, I must be having a phantom pregnancy' – all sorts of things went through my mind. Worst of all was that I couldn't calculate the date of my period because I hadn't had one, so I couldn't make plans to see Robert again. This was really awful. I decided not to say anything to Robert, not even to tell him I'd done the home pregnancy test. Better to wait and see – maybe, I prayed, it was just too early to tell.

And that's exactly what had happened: the hormones produced during pregnancy weren't yet at a high enough level to register on the home pregnancy testing kit. But I didn't know that at the time, and I was in a complete tizzy.

Finally the date arrived of what would have been my second period. It came and went, and still I hadn't started my period. Even then I tried not to build up my hopes, although I was getting more worked up all the time. I thought about all those women who spend years trying to get pregnant like this, and of how they manage to keep their sanity month after month. I told myself over and over again that a little bit of worry wasn't too bad but I mustn't overdo it. I couldn't think about anything else.

Finally, after five weeks had passed, I decided I must really, genuinely be pregnant. I phoned Robert to tell him.

'I'm absolutely *sure* I'm pregnant. It's been too long.'

Even now his reaction disappointed me – just the same old 'let's wait and see'. I think, like me, he was afraid of building up his hopes in case of disappointment. Robert asked me if I'd had a pregnancy test and I said I hadn't because I didn't want to admit to him the negative results I'd got. I said it was still a bit early for that.

A week later, however, I did another test and just couldn't make out whether the result was positive or negative. There seemed to be a brown ring in the bottom of the test tube, the positive indicator, but I thought perhaps I was seeing things I wanted to see. It was so faint you could hardly make it out.

I asked John what he thought but of course he wanted to see a brown ring as much as I did so I wouldn't have to sleep with Robert again. He was sure he saw it.

I still didn't know, so I went and bought another kit – and a week later I did another test. This time I could see another brown ring but it was still very faint so I still wasn't 100 per cent sure. With these kits you're always left in two minds as to whether you're pregnant or not. I wished so much that I could see a doctor, but of course that was impossible.

A day later I started feeling sick. The day after that I felt even sicker. Now there was no doubt in my mind. I knew I *had* to be pregnant whatever the test said.

Robert phoned and asked if I had done a test yet. I was just about to do another one, so I told him I'd phone him back in a couple of hours when I had the result.

I did it, and this time the result was pretty clearly positive. Not blaringly positive, but there was definitely a ring there. I phoned Robert back and told him.

'The test is positive. And I'm starting to get morning sickness too, and my breasts are swelling and getting tender. I know I'm pregnant, there's no doubt about it this time.'

To my astonishment, there was no jubilant reaction on the other end of the line.

'Oh good,' he said. 'We'll wait and see from now on then.' And that was all.

'Well, don't bounce around the room or anything,' I replied. I just couldn't understand his lukewarm reaction. I had expected him to say, 'Oh great, let's get together and crack open a bottle of champagne,' or something like that. But there was nothing from him, hardly a flicker.

However, I was pleased for myself, and immediately started calculating when it would be due. The date was early September, which made me happy because it meant I'd have time to recover before Christmas. Had it worked the first time I'd have been able to recover before the boys' summer holidays, but there was no point in thinking about that now.

The important thing was that I was pregnant, and things were really under way. I was happy about it even if Robert and Jean didn't seem to be. I knew that at some point it would dawn on them that they were going to get what they wanted more than anything else in the world, and then they would be as excited as I was. And I was very excited. I was a surrogate mother-to-be, bearing *their* child.

CHAPTER FIVE

The First Three Months

I WAS MUCH sicker during the first three months of this pregnancy than I had been in either of my others. They were almost trouble-free except for a little bit of backache and exhaustion. But those problems had arisen late in the other pregnancies. This time I started having morning sickness very early, and it was severe. Many days I couldn't even move because I felt so bad. I missed four weeks of work, and two days after I finally made it back, I got off the tube and promptly proceeded to vomit. That was one of the most embarrassing things that has ever happened to me, being sick at the station.

In a way I was half-pleased about being sick: it showed that there was a definite chemical change going on in my body, and somehow certified that I was genuinely pregnant. But that didn't make up for the physical devastation. I was sick from morning to night: I couldn't keep anything down, despite countless attempts at forcing myself to do so. Every time I looked at a plateful of food I felt sick, even though I was starving from not having eaten anything. Whenever I managed to get something down, it invariably insisted on coming right back up again.

After a while it got so bad that I wondered if I should give up my job sooner than I had been planning. I worked in town, and I didn't think I could make the long journey there and back every day.

The worst thing about the sickness was that there was no way of telling when it would end. I knew that it could carry on throughout the pregnancy, and that thought scared me to death. Sometimes I pictured myself weighing four or five stone by the time I had the baby.

The morning sickness made me feel so low that I couldn't cope with any emotional upset at all, and I got particularly upset over Robert's continuing lack of excitement. He had so totally prepared himself for disappointment that he couldn't or wouldn't accept that I was pregnant. There I was getting more excited and more positive almost daily, and the more I increasingly wanted and needed a positive response from Robert and Jean. Yet from Robert, through all this period, I got virtually nothing.

Jean did occasionally express her feelings. Once when I spoke to her on the phone she said, 'I'm so pleased.' It wasn't much, but it was something – and certainly more than I got from Robert. His attitude was always, 'Well, perhaps we should wait and see. You never know, something could go wrong.'

I felt like strangling the man! I thought, 'How can you have waited so long for this and still be so negative about it, so indifferent? Here I am jumping up and down on my chair with excitement trying to tell you that everything's all right, and all you can say is "wait and see, wait and see".' With each day that passed in those first weeks, I got more and more annoyed with him. Finally, when we were talking on the phone one day, I couldn't stand it any longer.

'For crying out loud,' I asked, 'aren't you pleased that this is happening? Don't you feel anything about it at all?'

Robert seemed a little shocked by my outburst, and he immediately arranged to have lunch with me. When we met he tried to set things right.

'Look, I have obviously upset you,' he said. 'What have I done, exactly?'

'It's not what you've done, it's what you *haven't* done!' I said. 'You're so indifferent to the whole thing. Here I am getting all excited about *your* baby and you don't seem to give a damn. Don't you want this baby? Is it only Jean that wants it? Don't you believe I'm genuinely pregnant? What's the problem?'

'Of course I believe you're pregnant,' he assured me. 'But I have been waiting to make absolutely sure. I just cannot risk building up my hopes, all of Jean's hopes, only to have them dashed by a miscarriage early in the pregnancy, or to find out that it's only tension that's delayed your period.'

I could understand that, and I told him so. But it did take a little while for it to sink in that he was telling the truth, and that I was expecting a more enthusiastic reaction than the situation deserved. I could see that perhaps we ought to be more cautious, more careful, that we should even expect a crash so we wouldn't be disappointed if something did happen.

But it was hard for me to think that way. It's just not in my nature. I couldn't say to him, 'Yes, Robert, you're right and I will restrain my enthusiasm from now on.' Because all the time I *was* happy, I *was* enthusiastic – and I was so happy that I could look forward to the pregnancy. I had confidence in myself being pregnant, and no fears about miscarriage. It had never happened before so there was no reason to suppose that it was going to happen now.

However rational I was about Robert's reaction, I felt bitterly disappointed and terribly alone.

The morning sickness created a practical problem for me. Orignally I had no intention of telling most people that I was pregnant until I couldn't wait any longer. That would have been at about the five-month mark, when I would have swollen perceptibly and people would start asking questions. Or they would say outright that I looked as if I was pregnant. I had known I would be having to confess at that point, and was prepared for it.

But the sickness threw everything off. I didn't know what

to do about it. For the first couple of weeks I told the neighbours that it was a 'flu bug, but after it had been going on for longer than that I got worried. If I waited much longer, and only talked about it when it was obvious anyway, people might begin to wonder. 'Why didn't she say anything before? She must have known she was pregnant long ago.' You can miss two periods, maybe three, before you wonder what's happening. You can bluff that away, but when you're vomiting all day and night, missing work, then there must be a reason for it, and people would expect you to realise you're pregnant – especially if you've been through it all before. The only thing I could do without arousing anyone's suspicions was to come out with it and tell people I thought I was pregnant.

I did this slowly, casually, just dropping hints by saying in an offhand way, 'Oh, I've missed my period, maybe I'm sick because I'm pregnant.' Then, in the following week or so, I started telling people that it was definite.

'Well, it looks as if we've had a little accident, and we'll be hearing the patter of another pair of tiny feet in nine months or so,' I told one of the neighbours. I felt that it was better this way, but it lengthened the time I would have to be on my guard and watch what I said.

It also meant that John had to be involved in the whole thing for longer than I had hoped and expected. Of course the neighbours all started ribbing him about it when they found out that 'we' were having another baby. He took the jokes well, like when his friends would say, 'Well, we can see what you've been up to then!' John doesn't get upset – you can tell easily from his face when he is. He took it in good humour, just shrugged it all off.

In other people's company I even made the sort of joke about it that they would expect me to make – things like, 'I didn't know anything about it, I was asleep at the time. It's all John's fault.' He would laugh along with the rest of them.

61

When we were on our own, John didn't comment very much on my being a surrogate mother. He did say, when I was about ten weeks pregnant, 'I don't really mind, but I don't want my mates to know about it.' He thought being the husband of a surrogate mother would make him look a fool in their eyes, and naturally he didn't want that. I could understand why. Most people aren't ready or willing to accept the idea of surrogate motherhood.

John was a little troubled by it too, I know. One time when I was talking about the baby, he said, 'That baby's half you. I don't like that.'

I shrugged. 'There's not much we can do about that now,' I said. He smiled. I think he was only playing. John's not someone who can show affection easily, and that was his way of doing it. He was not willing to let even this tiny part of me go away to somebody else. It wasn't really anything to do with the baby, in my opinion, just his way of showing he cared about me and didn't like the idea of sharing me with another man. But it did touch me.

*   *   *

Even though my morning sickness had forced me to tell all the neighbours that I was pregnant, I had still not planned to tell Betty and Jack, John's parents, until quite late in the pregnancy. I did feel a little anxious about them because Betty is a very sharp, intelligent woman. I was afraid that she might guess that something was up if I wasn't very careful, and I wanted plenty of time to work out what I was going to say. Fortunately we don't see much of them, because they live in Devon and only occasionally come up to London.

However, we were caught out. One day in early March, Jack and Betty announced that they were coming up to meet some old friends in town, and asked if they could spend the night at our house. That in itself presented no problem, as I was hardly showing at this point and could easily conceal my slight bulge under a pullover. I didn't have any worries about it at all, in fact.

But things didn't turn out the way I had planned. Betty and Jack arrived in the afternoon and we sat down to have tea together. As I sat back in the sofa, I said without thinking, 'Oh, my back aches.'

Betty looked at me and said, 'Maybe it's your period coming on.'

I was going to let it go at that, but my elder boy, who was sitting with us, piped up with another theory.

'Perhaps it's your baby, Mum,' he said in his innocent little voice.

For a moment there was a terrible silence, and I could feel my face going bright pink. Betty looked at me with a look of such puzzlement on her face that I almost burst out laughing. I had to do some quick thinking, so I jumped right in.

'Go play in the garden, boys,' I said. Jack tactfully took them out. As soon as they were gone, Betty turned to me.

'You're pregnant, are you?'

I nodded. 'Yes, I am. Three months.' She sat silently, waiting for me to go on.

'We haven't told you because the doctors say that there's something wrong with the baby's heart and there's a strong possibility that it won't survive. We didn't want to upset you, so we thought it would be better not to say anything yet.'

Betty's face was so filled with sorrow and compassion that I had to look away. I felt terrible for making her feel this way.

'Oh Kirsty darling,' she said. 'I'm so sad for you. But will it not die before then? How can it survive now?'

I had to take a deep breath before answering her.

'The doctors say the baby will live and thrive while it's in the womb. But once the cord is cut and it's on its own, it's very unlikely to manage. Its chances of survival are very slim.' The lie came out so easily, I felt ashamed of myself.

After I had told Betty this terrible news, the rest of their

63

stay was very subdued. When they were leaving, Betty gave me an extra hug.

'You're a brave girl, love,' she whispered in my ear.

Lying to Betty made me feel very bad. I had a hard time convincing myself that it was right to make John's parents suffer in this way. John felt it too. That night in bed he said how awful it was.

'I know it is,' I said. 'But it's necessary too. I don't know what else we could do.'

'Mum's quite broad-minded about most things,' John replied. 'She might well accept your being a surrogate mother if she knew all the facts.'

'Well,' I replied, 'she might do if it were another woman. But she would be sure to see this baby as another grandchild. It would be too close to home. I don't think she would be quite so broad-minded when it involved a baby coming from her son's wife. We really can't take the chance with her.'

In the end, John had to agree with me, even if he did so reluctantly. Lying made the whole thing much less complicated than it might be otherwise. And of course, now that we had started out telling them one thing, we couldn't change the story; we had to keep up the lie whether we liked it or not.

After that, whenever I spoke to Betty on the phone I made it clear that I didn't want to talk about the baby. She was very good about it all, very understanding, and didn't push me. But she did say at one point that if she were in my position, she would have had an abortion.

'I don't think it's fair to the baby,' she told me. 'To carry it to term like that just doesn't seem right.'

I was vague in my reply.

'It goes when it goes,' I said. Nothing more. I didn't want to get pressed into having a full discussion with her on the subject. Of course I agreed with her completely. If such a thing had happened, and the baby really didn't have a chance of surviving, I wouldn't have carried on with the

64

pregnancy. But as far as Betty was concerned, I felt differently about it, and didn't want to have an abortion.

One day around this time, a health visitor turned up out of the blue to see the boys. It was only a routine visit – she was attached to the doctor's surgery, and she had never seen the children before – but it gave me a bit of a shock. I wasn't very friendly to her. After my childhood experiences, I fear and mistrust anyone who has anything to do with the social services. And naturally I was alarmed at the thought that she might find out I was pregnant again. I prayed that I wouldn't vomit while she was there, but I couldn't kick up a fuss without setting off alarm bells in her head.

Luckily, everything went smoothly. She met the boys and chatted in the way they have of disguising the fact that they're looking you over, and after twenty minutes she got up to leave – blissfully ignorant of the truth. Apparently she was satisfied with what she saw, because she said there would be no need for her to visit again.

I kept thinking how lucky I was that she had come now and not in a few months' time, when it would be obvious that I was pregnant. The fact that a new baby was on the way would have gone into her records, and I certainly did not want my doctor to know about it. Imagine how the health visitor would have reacted if she had known what was going on!

I still had to sort out doctors with Robert and Jean, but I didn't feel there was a pressing need to do this until I was three months gone or thereabouts.

Needless to say, the boys had no idea of the real circumstances of the pregnancy, but at about ten weeks I realised that it was time to tell them I was going to have another baby. They didn't seem all that interested, and simply went back to what they had been doing before.

In the days and weeks that followed, however, they started taking a normal childish interest in it. There was one funny time when some cats were yowling in the street and the older boy said, 'Mummy, I can hear your baby crying.' I didn't have the heart to tell him that he couldn't possibly hear it, so I carried on letting him think he had. Later they wanted to feel the baby moving, and when they sat on my lap, they wondered if they were sitting on the baby. 'Am I hurting the baby when I sit here?' they would ask.

I had been very worried about what to tell them after the birth. They were bound to have trouble understanding why the baby hadn't come home, but I thought that, since they were so young, perhaps they would accept the situation more readily than older children might.

In the end I decided that the easiest way of explaining it would be to say that the baby had died, and I hoped they would accept that and not worry about it for too long. I knew that there might be problems, and I would have to be on the lookout for them so that I could put the boys' minds at rest. But I was pretty sure that, being so young, they would briefly wonder why Mummy hadn't brought the baby home, and then forget about it after a few weeks.

*　　*　　*

I was beginning to find it a terrible strain not to be able to tell anyone about my secret. My friend Carol, the only person apart from John who knew about it, was still in Germany with her husband and children. With her gone, I didn't have anyone else to confide in, and I missed her a lot. The continuing coolness of Robert and Jean surprised and hurt me, and it compounded the difficulty of not having anyone to talk to.

When I was nearly three months pregnant, I decided I absolutely *had* to have someone else to talk to. There was really only one other person who might understand, and that was my friend Linda.

I met Linda on a secretarial course some years ago, and we quickly became great friends. We got married and had children at around the same time, and since then we've shared some very private things. Linda lives in a different part of London but we see each other quite a lot, usually once a week. In all that time, however, I hadn't breathed a word to her about running backwards and forwards to hotels, and sleeping with a strange man! And I hadn't seen her during the worst of my morning sickness.

Now I knew I had to tell her. Even if Linda didn't completely approve of what I was doing, I thought that she might accept the situation and help me out. I rang her up one day and made a date to go and see her with my boys the following Saturday.

Linda has two children, a boy and girl, and they get along very well with my children. When the two of us get together we pack them off to play and settle down for a chat. This time was no different: the children all went out into the garden to play, and Linda and I sat in her kitchen having a cup of tea.

We had been talking about this and that, our children and schools and that sort of thing, when I abruptly changed the subject.

'Have you got a deep dark secret?' I asked. 'Something you're too frightened or too embarrassed to tell anybody, but that you dearly want to confess?'

Linda thought a moment.

'No,' she replied, 'not really. But obviously you have.'

'Well, yes,' I said.

Linda smiled.

'Go on then,' she said. 'You can tell me. You're not pregnant, are you?'

I was a little taken aback by that, but thought it must simply have been a good guess.

'Uh, yes, as a matter of fact I am.'

'Well,' replied Linda, 'if that's not the secret, then the only thing I can guess is that it's not your husband's baby.'

In my nervousness, I giggled like a schoolgirl. I was amazed by her perceptiveness.

'How the hell did you know that?' I demanded.

She shrugged. 'I didn't, really. It's just that you've seemed preoccupied for a long time, for weeks in fact, and I thought at first that I'd upset you or offended you in some way. But after what you've just said, I realise that there must be something else behind it. You must be worried about something else. The only thing I know at the moment is that you're pregnant, so if there's a deep dire secret, or if you think of it that way, then it must be because the baby isn't John's.'

I paused, still a little stunned.

'Yes, you're quite right,' I finally said. 'It's not his.' And I paused again. I didn't know what to say next.

Linda took up the thread for me.

'Well,' she said, 'if it's not his, then whose is it?'

I was frightened. Even though I had wanted to talk to her about this, I wasn't sure if I could go ahead with it. But she was looking at me with great interest now, and I could see there was no turning back. I plunged in.

'Well, that's actually the deep dark secret. It's not so much who the father is, as what my relationship is with him.'

I could see that Linda no more understood what I was driving at than if I'd said I was pregnant by a frog prince. She was looking back at me with questioning eyes. I took a deep breath and spoke again.

'Have you ever heard of surrogate mothers?'

'No,' replied Linda.

So I explained what a surrogate mother was, and Linda caught on immediately. She leaned forward over the table where we were sitting and said, 'Don't tell me, you mean you're a surrogate mother, and the baby is...'

'That's right,' I said. 'I'm having the baby for another couple.'

There was silence for a few long moments, then Linda just said, 'Well, well, well.'

There was silence again, this time for a minute at least. I wanted to let Linda digest this very strange information.

Finally I asked her, 'How do you feel about me, now you know?'

Linda shook her head.

'It really doesn't make any difference to me,' she replied. 'It doesn't affect me in any way. Why should it?'

'Well, most people would be pretty shocked, I think. Probably pretty disgusted. They think that any woman who can "give away" a child she's given birth to is some kind of terrible ogre. I have wanted to tell you about this for so long, but I was worried that you would disapprove. I've only told you now because I thought you were open-minded enough to be, well not necessarily *for* it, but at least that you would accept the situation.'

Linda was emphatic in her reply.

'Oh, I *do* accept it,' she said. 'I accept the situation totally. I don't feel any differently towards you now than I did yesterday. You're not a terrible ogre, you're my friend, and that's that. Anyway, I'm happy to know that I haven't done something to annoy you. Honestly, that's what I was worried about, seeing you so preoccupied.'

I can't describe how relieved I was at what Linda said. It was so silly: I had been worried that she would think I was some kind of freak, and she had been worried that she had offended me! Now that I had had the courage to tell somebody, and my judgement of her character had been correct, I was elated. In fact, after my dire confession, I felt like hugging her and kissing her and thanking her for continuing to be my friend. When you do something like I was doing, little voices inside begin to say what you're doing really is not normal. Linda's reaction showed me that it wasn't that way at all, and I'll always be grateful to her for that support.

Even more important to me at that moment was the thought that at least I would have someone to talk to about it, someone in whom I could confide. I didn't expect her to help me or advise me if she didn't want to, but at least I could talk to someone other than John – who wasn't really interested most of the time – or Robert and Jean. They had their own worries and didn't want me to put any pressure on them.

So it was great knowing that Linda was there, and throughout the pregnancy she helped me a lot. Whenever I saw her she checked up on how things were progressing – whether I had found a doctor yet, what the antenatal care was like, how the baby felt. She never kept on about it, she just slipped in these little questions so that she knew how I was doing.

Linda had a very clever method, actually. We would be talking about the usual subjects, children and shopping and all the other things that mothers usually yack about, and then suddenly, out of nowhere, would come a very direct question.

'How did you actually get pregnant?'

'How many times did you have to try before it worked?'

'Do you like the people you're having the baby for?'

She would ask the question and then, as soon as I'd answered, she changed the subject and appeared to forget about it. She would carry on talking about something else, but then later, maybe a half-hour later, she would slip in another question, and when she had heard the answer to that one she would go on to another topic. In this way she learned a lot about the pregnancy and my relationship with Robert and Jean. This was great, exactly what I wanted. She didn't pry or spy, she just let me know she was interested by dropping in those questions. (And she also managed to keep up with the gossip, which I suppose was pretty good.) She had the best of both worlds: helping me and finding out about everything at the same time.

Up until the time I told Linda, not being able to talk to anyone had been a terrible strain. It's still hard, even now, because there is hardly anyone I can talk to about it. I suppose it's a little bit like being a homosexual and not

70

wanting everyone to know about it. Certain people know, so you can be open and comfortable with them, but with most you have to keep it a secret. And that deceit is not only distasteful, it's very hard to keep up. For one thing, you have to have a damned good memory so you remember who knows and who doesn't. Every day you have to be on your guard against slips. You think, 'Right, she knows about it so I can talk to her and don't have to tell lies.' But then an hour later you see someone else who doesn't know, so you have to go back to keeping up the act.

Foremost in my mind was that I couldn't mention Robert and Jean in front of them or let them hear me phoning Robert and Jean. In many ways, this was the worst aspect of the whole experience.

*　　*　　*

At twelve weeks, I was beginning to show. And for some reason, I began developing all sorts of maternal feelings.

These upset me quite a bit: I was frightened of how they would develop, whether they would grow and get worse as the weeks went by. I found myself thinking about how, afterwards, I'd have another baby to replace the one I was going to give up.

For a week or so the maternal feelings overwhelmed me, and I thought quite seriously about having another baby with John. I told him that, despite what I'd always said in the past about not wanting any more children, I thought that maybe I had changed my mind and wanted another one after all. I explained that having another baby might be a good idea just in case I had been storing up maternal feelings and was unable to satisfy them. It might make it easier for me to get rid of the frustrations and make being a surrogate mother easier as well, although, when the time came, I might find that I didn't want another baby after all. I used to keep up this love-talk with him, saying silly things like 'One of your

71

little sperm ought to pay a visit to one of my little eggs and you never know what might happen.'

I'm not sure that John actually wanted another baby, but I know he was pleased and flattered, especially after the rocky period we had been through during the couple of years before. And funnily enough, we were now getting on very well. John was being very supportive of me and what I was doing, and we seemed to have been drawn closer by it all.

But I knew that I would be letting myself in for big trouble if I continued having such strong maternal feelings towards this baby. And when they did not disappear, I decided I had to do something about them. So I made a deliberate mental effort to become more detached from the baby inside my womb. It was very difficult; there were times when I thought I couldn't do it. But I forced myself to. I started thinking about the baby inside me as belonging by moral right to someone else, rather than to me. It was Robert and Jean's responsibility, not mine.

Slowly, thank goodness, the detachment grew and I began to master my maternal feelings. I was very happy about this, even though it was painful in many ways. It had frightened me when I started thinking about having another baby to replace this one.

By the beginning of the thirteenth week I didn't feel so strongly about having another baby. I thought that maybe I would like one some time in the future, before I was too old to have any more, but the need felt much less pressing and less painful. This pleased me: I didn't want another baby of my own to be connected even in my feelings with the baby I was carrying for Robert and Jean. Looking back, I think that I was going through a crisis about what I was doing. My success in detaching myself was a sign that I was coming to terms with it.

*   *   *

It was all very well for me to be detached from the baby, but I was fed up with Robert and Jean's detachment from me. In those early months they hardly ever rang me up as they used to, and that really upset me. One weekend, when I was around eleven weeks pregnant, I decided I had to let them know about how I was feeling. When I phoned, my voice must have been noticeably edgy and uptight, because Robert asked me almost straightaway what the matter was.

'I'm disappointed in this whole thing,' I told him.

'Disappointed in what sense?' he asked. He sounded a little alarmed.

'Well, it's just not what I expected. I thought we were going to be good friends while this was happening, that we were going to share the pregnancy and everything else. And now I feel as if the relationship is growing colder instead of warmer. This isn't what I wanted, and it's worrying me.'

Robert didn't agree.

'Nothing's changed for us,' he reassured me. 'As far as we're concerned, we're all friends; everything is just the same as it was before.'

After that, I decided not to press the issue. I admitted that I had been having confusing feelings about the whole thing – though I didn't say exactly what they were, because I didn't want him and Jean to start worrying about whether I would hand over the baby in the end. I said that I was probably over-reacting because of my hormones or something, and left it at that. Robert didn't make any effort to prove me wrong.

That shut me up, anyway. I wasn't going to force myself into places where someone else thought I didn't belong. I had too much pride for that.

I think that this was when I realised I might not get what I had wanted from surrogate motherhood in the first place. After all the meetings and phone calls before I actually got pregnant, Robert's and Jean's reticence was a sudden change, and hard to deal with.

But I had been worrying too much, and forgetting what

they must have been going through too. After all, they were guarding against disappointment all the time. They had seen too much of it before. And in any case, to my delight, their attitude soon underwent an abrupt change.

Shortly after the three-month mark had passed, Robert phoned me. He said that he and Jean had been talking things over, and they both knew that now the chances of miscarriage were much lower. And in light of that, they thought it was as safe as it would ever be for Jean to raise her hopes a little bit. She could, he thought, start meeting me and enjoying the pregnancy with me. I was very pleased about that.

On a more practical level, I also thought it was about time I registered with a doctor. The idea was to do this through Robert and Jean. When he suggested that the three of us meet up for lunch, my own hopes were raised. Now perhaps we could relax and be friends.

And at last Robert made his first real acknowledgement of my pregnancy by saying that when we met, he would give me the first payment of £1,000 – 10 per cent of the total we had agreed. I felt disappointed that the money had to come first as far as he was concerned, but any positive acknowledgement was a step forward. And it was early days yet.

CHAPTER SIX

Finding a Doctor

WE MET FOR lunch a few days later in a pub by the river. It was mid-March but the weather was mild and sunny, the sort of weather that puts almost everyone in a good mood. It certainly did wonders for all of us. We got on well, with hardly any tensions or conflicts arising the whole afternoon.

This was the first time I had seen Jean since we discussed conception months earlier, though I had chatted to her on the phone a number of times, of course. She was quiet but very friendly, and I often noticed her shyly glancing at my stomach. She was much more relaxed than usual.

Robert too seemed relaxed, far more so than I had seen him before. Perhaps it was because the three-month period was over and he could let Jean become involved now. He didn't even seem to mind giving me my first payment, handing it to me without any comment except 'Here you are – you can count it if you want!' But he said it in a jokey, friendly way.

Our easiness together made me very happy. I realised how much I liked both Robert and Jean. Apart from occasional bouts of nausea, my morning sickness had stopped, so I was settling down to enjoy the pregnancy. Now I was enjoying their company as well, and feeling for the first time that we were all friends.

Robert and Jean were in the middle of moving house, and were full of stories about their new home. Like me, Jean is a really enthusiastic homemaker, and we had a lot to talk about. When we eventually got onto the subject of the pregnancy, the first thing they brought up was getting a doctor. They wanted me to contact their GP as soon as possible.

This had all been planned from the beginning. Robert and Jean were fortunate in having a kindly GP who had seen Jean through all her years of infertility tests and invest-igations, and they had confided in him early on that they were thinking of trying to find a surrogate mother to have Robert's baby. They told me that the doctor had been very sympathetic, wished them luck, and said he was always available if they needed him. They had inferred from this that he would be willing to look after any woman they found to have the baby for them.

Knowing this had put me very much at ease. I knew I had to have proper antenatal care, and since my pregnancy had to be kept a secret from my own doctor, I had to use someone else. Their doctor was fine with me. I was very happy that I wouldn't have to find another one on my own, in addition to all the other practical problems I had. My main concern was to ensure that I didn't fall ill or have to take one of my own sons to our GP while I was obviously pregnant, but John said that he would take the boys to the doctor if necessary.

We also talked again about my having the baby at their home. We had agreed on this from the beginning, thinking it would be easier to hand over the baby after a home birth. Then afterwards, I thought, I would have my postnatal care somewhere else. If I were to tell everyone that the baby had been stillborn it would seem reasonable to have postnatal care at my own home, but I didn't want any of the local midwives to be involved. It wasn't worth the risk.

In the same way, I didn't want my GP to know because he is a Roman Catholic and wouldn't have taken kindly to what we were doing. I felt sure that he would strongly disapprove.

So dealing with Robert and Jean's GP seemed by far the

best course of action. When they suggested I ring him I agreed happily, and said I would make an appointment the next day. At 10 a.m. on the following Tuesday I trotted off to see him.

The surgery was a clinic with several doctors, and Robert and Jean's GP was a very kindly man in his mid-forties. But his sympathetic demeanour dropped pretty quickly when I told him why I was there.

To my astonishment, he told me that Robert and Jean had entirely misunderstood what he had said to them. I suppose that he had never really imagined they would find a surrogate mother, but, in any case, if they thought that he would serve as the doctor if they did find one, they had been wrong. It was completely out of the question. He was under no obligation to take me on, he said, and he certainly was not going to. He apologised for the misunderstanding, but made it perfectly clear that there was no arguing with him. I would have to find another doctor.

I walked away from the clinic in shock and turmoil. I had gone there expecting sympathy and understanding, and what I got instead was tacit disapproval.

I was also deeply alarmed. We were back to square one as far as doctors were concerned, and I didn't have the faintest idea how I was going to find another one. With me in my fourteenth week of pregnancy, it was rather late to be looking now. And I was very upset that I would have to find one myself after all. I rang Robert and Jean to tell them the bad news.

I spoke to Robert, who was very confused at first. Then he became angry.

'I'm *sure* he said he would help us,' he kept insisting. 'This is ridiculous.'

'Well, it may be ridiculous,' I replied, 'but it's true. He's not going to take me on, so there's no point in going on about it. We'll have to find another doctor. And soon.'

I realised that before we could even start looking, there

were lots of little things I had to work out. The most important was the story I would tell. I couldn't just walk into the surgery and say, 'Hi, I'm a surrogate mother and I need a GP. Would you like to help?' I had to invent something.

After talking it over with Robert and Jean, I decided what the story would be. In some respects it really wasn't all that far from the truth.

I would tell the doctor that I was a married woman who had been having an affair with a married man. I had become pregnant by him, and had originally wanted to have an abortion. But the father I would say, wanted to keep the baby, and I had agreed to this. I didn't want to have the baby in my own area, because I didn't want my own GP or my neighbours to know about it, so I had been forced to go elsewhere. This seemed a reasonable story, and I set about seeing if it would wash.

It didn't. I spent two whole days trekking from doctor to doctor telling my story, and none of them would have anything to do with me. Most of those I visited were in Robert and Jean's area, and I phoned many others to see if they would co-operate. None would.

One of the objections that all the doctors raised was that I wanted to have a home birth, and moreover a concealed birth of sorts. None of them wanted to be involved in that. They refused to take me on.

After a few days of this I was fed up and extremely worried. I phoned Robert to tell him what was going on.

I explained what had happened, and said that I just didn't know what to do. 'Time is running out,' I concluded, 'and I'm at my wit's end.'

To my annoyance and outrage, he was completely unhelpful. He coolly informed me that it wasn't his problem.

'You ought to be talking to Jean about this,' he said. 'It's her problem, and yours. It's really nothing to do with me.' He had enough worries of his own at work, and the baby was our business. He could sympathise with the hard time I was having finding a doctor, and knew that I was pregnant and having 'hormone changes' and everything. But that, he repeated, was a problem for Jean and me to sort out. We should get on with it and leave him alone.

His attitude upset me incredibly. I couldn't understand how he could be so detached and uncaring. The whole business seemed trivial to him. If I wanted to sort things out then I should do it, but he had other things to worry about.

I was furious, but I was also level-headed enough to know that if I didn't persevere I would never find a GP in time, and then I'd be in real trouble.

So it was back to the telephone.

Eventually, after a few more days of failure and frustration and tears, I found someone who was sympathetic. She was a young woman GP and she was at least willing to listen to my case.

The more I talked, the more I began thinking that I had found the answer to my problem. She was very sympathetic, asking questions about the supposed father and whether I was sure I wanted to go ahead with it, and so forth. She really seemed to care about my well-being and didn't instantly dismiss me the way so many others had. Finally, at the end, she agreed in principle to take me on as her patient.

There was only one catch, and that was that she would not agree if the baby was to be born at home. It had to be a hospital birth. By this time it had become clear to me that the home-birth idea was impossible and impractical, so I can't say I was surprised when she told me this. I agreed, knowing Robert and Jean and I would have to adjust our plans accordingly, but I was so happy to find a sympathetic doctor that I didn't mind that. I made an appointment to see her in a few days.

My first appointment was a shock. Having told her the story in brief over the telephone, I arrived to discover that I was going to have to tell it again in detail.

I was quite emotional that day, crying all the time that I told her the story. This is not like me, but I suppose that the strain of not finding a doctor - followed by the relief of finding her - had really got to me. Now, confronted with her probing questions, I had to let myself go: it was all too much for me.

I was also feeling pressure from my uncertainty about whether the doctor would take me on. Even though she had said she would, after all the disappointment with the other doctors I couldn't be sure. And I hoped, of course, that I'd be able to keep up the deception long enough to convince her.

So there I was, recounting my tale of woe and crying like a baby, genuine tears flooding down my cheeks the whole time.

The story, as I told it to the doctor, was this.

My husband had been abroad for a year on business, and while he was gone I had had an affair with another man. I said the affair was not serious: I didn't love this man and I did love my husband. I didn't want to leave him. Nor, to begin with, did I want to have the baby. But the father wanted it because his wife was infertile and couldn't have a baby of her own. When he learned I was pregnant he had begged me not to have an abortion but to carry it to term, and then hand it over to him and his wife. When my husband came back, the baby would already have been born and I would be able to act as if nothing had happened. I explained that I wanted to make the wife of my 'boyfriend' happy, but that I couldn't risk hurting my husband, and I would have to have an abortion if I didn't find a doctor who would take me on.

The doctor seemed to approve of my not wanting to have an abortion, but she was concerned about whether I would be able to give up the baby when it was born. I told her very emphatically that I could and would - that I wouldn't be doing this if I thought that was a problem.

As I told the story, my tears slowly dried up and I think that I convinced the doctor of my determination. By the end, she seemed persuaded that I knew what I was doing, and I felt secure in the knowledge that what I had told her was confidential. Even if she hadn't believed me, she could not check anything without my permission. As it was, she did not ask to see Robert to verify my account of things.

Having accepted that I would have to have the baby in hospital, I planned to stay the minimum six hours and then leave, as long as there weren't any complications. The doctor said that there would be a shared care arrangement between the hospital and herself for antenatal care. But she was worried about my postnatal care; she wondered where I was going to go. Lying, I suggested that I could stay at the house with my 'boyfriend' and his wife. The doctor didn't think that was a very good idea. She thought it would be too great a strain on me to stay in the same house as the baby after the birth.

I told her that I had no place else to go: I daren't go home, because my neighbours are friends with the local midwives and they were bound to get wind of what was going on. I could not go to my own GP because my husband was likely to find out about it. (That, after all, was my reason for coming to her rather than my own GP in the first place.) The truth was that I hadn't really worked it all through. I was saying that I'd stay at Robert and Jean's, but I had no intention whatsoever of doing that.

Suddenly I had a bright idea. I suggested to the doctor that, after leaving the baby in the hospital, perhaps I might be able to stay at a hotel instead. She seemed to think that was perfectly reasonable, and perhaps the best solution of all. The midwives could come to see me there, and no one in my neighbourhood need know where I was. It might be a bit lonely, but what else could I do?

What I didn't tell the doctor was exactly how I'd fit in the hotel with my real plans. My friend Linda would bring the boys up to see me: they'd be told it was a hospital, and being so young they would believe that. I knew that it would be great to see them then.

The bad part of this plan (which the doctor couldn't

know, of course) was that I wouldn't be able to see John for ten days or two weeks. You never know when the midwives are going to turn up, and if they turned up while he was visiting, they would start to wonder who this strange man was. And they don't make appointments – probably because they always like to try and catch you doing something you're not supposed to do, like being up and about too soon. It could so easily happen that John and the boys were there when the midwives arrived, and the boys would automatically call John 'Daddy', and the midwives would naturally be suspicious. I could have tried telling them a different version of the story, but that would be much too risky. It would be safer if John didn't come to the hotel at all.

This would make me miserable, but I tried to look on the bright side, telling myself that I would be able to use that time alone to recover emotionally as best I could. I could do all my crying and get it out of my system before I went home. I wondered if Robert and Jean would come and see me while I was there.

The doctor made an appointment for me at the antenatal clinic of the local hospital and said that she would write a letter for me to take there. She told me to come and see her to pick up the letter before my first appointment.

I went home feeling relieved. Although we suddenly had some unexpected complications about the aftercare, it was just as well that they had come up now and not later. And I felt confident that we could work around them. In some ways the idea of staying in a hotel after the birth appealed to me, despite the loneliness I thought I would feel there.

That evening I rang Robert and told him what had happened with the doctor.

'Oh, fine,' he said. But I could tell from his tone of voice that he was not very pleased about it. I guessed that he was worried about the hotel bill. Though we didn't actually talk about it, it was tacitly understood that he would be the one to pay it. But Jean, I thought, was probably pleased that she would get the baby to herself immediately, without having to share it with me. And that side of it was fine with me, too. I wanted her to feel that the baby was hers from the very start.

The following week I went back to the doctor to pick up my letter. She had obviously been thinking about the situation in the meantime, and she seemed to be even more on my side than she had been before. She talked about Robert as if he were some sort of terrible person for having done this to me. But she still had some reservations about the whole thing, she said, and most of the time she just fired a whole load of questions at me.

Did I really know what I was doing? she asked. Was I going to tell my husband about it eventually, or keep it from him forever? Did I realise that the baby might turn up wanting to meet me in twenty-five years? How would I feel then if my husband didn't know anything about it?

Most of these questions I had not anticipated, and I had to do some pretty quick thinking while the interrogation was going on. I said that my husband and I had already planned to go on holiday together when he returned from his year overseas, and that I had decided to tell him everything then. That would at least prevent any shocks later on, and would mean that I didn't have to keep this a secret from him. And I said that if the child wanted to meet me in twenty years or whatever, I'd welcome it into my home and explain exactly why I did what I had done. I hoped I was making the right decision, and I really did think I was. I'd have to tell my own children then what had happened as well, but by then they would be young men and I hoped that they would understand.

All this made my doctor feel much better. And I, too, felt much less nervous than I had my first time at the surgery, even though I was on the edge of my seat throughout my improvised storytelling.

The doctor did point out one problem that I had not been aware of, and it was a good thing that she did. She said she understood my need for secrecy and speed, but after thinking about my intention of walking out of the hospital after six hours, leaving the baby behind, she had realised that this would present a problem. If I did leave the baby there, it would be classified as abandoned and would automatically become a ward of court. That meant immediately being taken into care by the local authority, and obviously I didn't want that to happen.

Apparently this would be the case even if the father and I were married, so Robert would have even less of a chance! He would not be able to go in and pick up the baby for me. The doctor also said that if I did leave the hospital without the baby, I'd have a great deluge of social workers trying to make me keep it.

I nearly panicked when she told me this. Everything seemed to be crashing down on us. I asked her how we could get around the problem, if there was any way at all.

She replied that the only way round it was to take the baby with me when I left. I should go with it to the hotel and have my ten days of postnatal care there. This would be traumatic for me, but far less traumatic, she thought, than having to put up with all the red tape and the pressure from social services.

At this point she asked me again if I was sure I wanted to go through with the plan.

'It's not too late to change your mind, you know,' she said. 'There are other alternatives you could choose.'

I was still feeling a bit panicky but I told her I thought I could cope. I said I was becoming more and more detached from the baby – which happened to be true – and that I thought this would continue. I said I'd invite Jean round to feed and change the baby as soon as possible, so I would keep the detached feeling up even after it was born.

'I know it's not going to be easy, but I also think this is the best way. But I appreciate your concern, I really do.'

'I'm just trying to help you make the right decision for

yourself and for the baby,' she replied.

'I know, thank you, really.' I didn't know what more to say.

The doctor then handed me the letter she had written to take to the antenatal clinic. It wasn't sealed, and while the doctor was out of the room for a moment I took it out of the envelope and read it.

To my astonishment, I saw that this wasn't just a standard booking-in letter. She had told the consultant the whole story. When she came back in the room I waved the letter at her.

'Why do you have to go into all the details?' I demanded.

She seemed annoyed that I had opened the letter, but didn't get angry with me.

'I thought that the hospital should know this is not an ordinary case,' she said in a quiet voice.

I'm afraid I got rather heated in my reply.

'But you and I know that,' I said. 'Why does the hospital have to know as well? They're so nosey these days – so many things they want you to do or don't want you to do. And you said yourself that the social workers would be all over me if anything "unusual" was going on. Why can't they just leave women in peace to have their babies the way they want to? You can't give birth at home, you can't do anything the way you want to do it!'

Even in my anger I could see that the doctor was a little taken aback by my outburst. But she spoke very calmly when she answered.

'I feel,' she said, 'that I have a social obligation towards your child as well as a medical one. I have to do what's best for the whole situation, not just for your physical health.'

That really got me.

'Social obligation! What danger is this baby in, anyway? If I was a drunkard, and I was married to a man who beat me up and who was on the dole, and I had six other kids and was pregnant again, then there would *really* be some problems –

but if everything was "normal" because I planned to keep the baby, there wouldn't be anything the hospital could do to stop me taking it home to a lousy environment. Well, is that better than this situation? Just because the woman wants to keep her baby, does that mean she's normal? My case may be bizarre, but the baby's going to a very affluent couple, and it's going to have a very good upbringing. Surely that's the important thing!'

I don't know how the doctor felt about getting a lecture from this irate character on all the finer points of medical ethics, but she seemed to accept my argument. In any case, she agreed to give me an ordinary booking-in letter. She had it typed up right then and there, so that I could take it away with me from the surgery. When I had calmed down a little, I apologised for my outburst and told her again how much I appreciated what she was doing for me. She told me to ring her any time I needed to, and off I went.

I was all set.

I felt pretty good now about the medical side of things. The doctor was essentially on my side, despite her reservations, and she had agreed to do most things in the way I wanted them done.

I was particularly grateful that she had pointed out the problems that would have arisen had I handed over the baby in the hospital. That would have been a disaster for everyone.

Still, it would be tough on Robert and Jean not getting the baby straightaway. I had to keep it with me at the hotel for the ten days of postnatal care, otherwise things would look suspicious. That meant that they would have to wait for all that time before taking it home with them. And the delay might compound any fears they had about my not handing it over to them. After all, the more contact I had with it, the more likely I was to become attached to it. This worried me a little bit too: after spending all that time with the baby, I might have difficulty parting with it. I really did not want to become too attached to it.

I rang Robert and Jean that evening to let them know what had happened with the doctor. I told them what she had said about the danger of leaving the baby at the hospital for Robert to pick up, and said that if I was going to take the baby to the hotel they wouldn't be able to have it for ten days, rather than the four days we had planned on.

I knew they wouldn't like this, but I was very firm. There was no way I was going to get involved in a legal battle for them to get custody from the local authority. Everything would come out in the open if that happened, and all the bureaucrats would want to know every detail. In any case, Robert and Jean wouldn't be able to do anything about it, since legally the baby was mine and they had no claim on it. I implied that if they wanted to make a fuss they could, but it wouldn't get them anywhere. And I didn't want to get involved.

They really had no choice, and they knew it. They agreed immediately on the telephone without protesting. But they wanted to talk more about it, so we made a date to have dinner the next night.

At dinner, they dropped a bombshell.

'We don't want you to stay at a hotel,' Jean told me. 'We want you to stay with us.'

This shocked me. I'd got used to the idea of being at a hotel for the ten days of postnatal care and did not want to feel 'trapped' at their house, on their ground. The hotel seemed the obvious and most simple course of action. At the same time, Jean's explanation of their plan made a lot of sense.

'It will be easier for both of us,' she said. 'The hotel would be so lonely and anonymous, and if you stay at our house then I'll have twenty-four-hour contact with the baby from the start – except when the midwives come round, naturally.'

I objected at first, explaining all my reasons for preferring the hotel. For one thing, it would help me heal physically. I'd be having to take a couple of salt baths a day, and I'd feel embarrassed about doing this at Robert's and Jean's. Also, I wouldn't have to worry about food at the hotel. When I mentioned this, Jean countered by saying that she would wait on me hand and foot; I would have a television and radio in the room and all my meals brought to me.

'It will be just like a hotel,' she joked, 'but the food will be a lot better.'

I laughed, but pointed out that I would feel embarrassed having her wait on me. You're not exactly an invalid when you've had a baby: it's simply a matter of preference to want to laze around for a while afterwards.

'Do you know what you're taking on?' I asked her. 'Both a newborn baby and the person who's just given birth to it – that's quite a lot to look after!'

Jean was quite sure that she could cope, and both she and Robert would much prefer doing it this way. I wasn't sure about Robert's motives in this new plan. I suspected strongly that what really worried him was paying the bill for a ten-day stay at a hotel. But I understood Jean's point of view at any rate, and I came round before long.

'Well,' I finally said, 'I suppose that will be all right. But I'll be wanting to phone my husband pretty often, and I don't want to have to ask if I can use the phone all the time.'

'That won't be a problem,' said Robert. 'You can have a phone in your room and use it whenever you want.' I was happy to hear that, and felt slightly silly for raising such an unimportant point right there and then. But you never know about these things until you come out and ask.

With this new arrangement I knew that I wouldn't be able to see my boys for those ten days. If they heard the baby crying at Robert's and Jean's, they would want to know if it was my baby. And when they couldn't go to see it, they would get confused and upset. So I thought the best plan would be to send them off to their grandparents for ten days.

The thought of not seeing them made me a little tearful – I would miss them so much, especially then. But I knew it would be better this way. Their grandparents wouldn't mind, and they wouldn't find it unusual because it was natural enough not to want to see anyone when you've had a stillborn child. And ten days would pass very quickly, at least for the boys. I didn't know what that time would be like for me...

Once the arrangements were all agreed and everyone seemed happy with them, things got a little easier between Robert and Jean and me. Working out the mechanics had certainly proved far more difficult than any of us would have anticipated.

Even now, with everything planned down to the last detail, we all realised that some surprise could pop up and throw all our plans into disarray. For instance, any complications with the pregnancy – anything that required more than the ordinary medical care – could throw a huge spanner into the works. But for the time being, things were pretty well settled, and I wasn't going to worry about problems until the problems actually arose.

I can't say that I was really happy about staying with Robert and Jean. The knowledge that I wouldn't see John and the boys for all that time made me very unhappy; I could hardly bear thinking about it. But I could see that there were certain advantages. I would be able to help Jean if she wanted, to show her how to care for the baby and give the sort of advice that I had once needed myself. That would make it more bearable, if nothing else. And, after all, I had been the one who wanted a close relationship with them. Nothing could be closer than this – first sharing the pregnancy and then staying with the parents and their new baby in the home where they would all be living together. I suppose I couldn't complain, really.

CHAPTER SEVEN

4–6 Months

I HAD MY first appointment at the antenatal clinic when I was fourteen weeks pregnant. I was glad to go, to check that everything was going all right and the baby was growing normally. The doctor was a nice woman who told me that everything was fine. She ticked me off for smoking and I promised to cut down as much as possible if I couldn't stop completely. I knew I couldn't give up my five cigarettes a day, and Robert and Jean had never expressed any concern about this, so I thought that keeping the number down was at least something.

The doctor also insisted that I was sixteen weeks pregnant and not fourteen! Doctors always know they're right so I didn't argue, but of course I knew she had it wrong. In this particular instance, there was no possibility that the doctor could know better than I did when I had conceived.

That evening I rang Robert and Jean to let them know that the baby was fine. I hoped that the news would encourage them to be more openly pleased than they had been up till then. Robert answered the phone, and I told him the news. I also joked in passing about the doctor's miscalculation, and was surprised by his reaction.

'But if the doctor is right,' he said, 'and you are sixteen weeks pregnant, then the baby can't be mine.'

I could hardly believe my ears.

'You're as bad as the doctor!' I snapped. 'I think I should know who the father is, Robert, and it's you. If it was my husband's baby, *my* baby, I wouldn't even contemplate letting you have it.'

I calmed down and tried to explain. 'Look,' I said, 'all babies grow at different rates, just as they do later in their lives. So it's perfectly normal for the foetus to seem larger or smaller than average at any stage in the pregnancy.'

There was silence on the other end of the line. I almost lost my temper completely.

'For God's sake!' I spluttered. 'Do you still not believe me? If you really have doubts about who the father is, why don't you have a blood test done when the baby is born? Then there'll be no doubt.'

Robert said something to indicate that he wasn't really worried, but I felt wounded that he couldn't even trust me to keep one of the most important parts of our agreement: not to have sexual intercourse with John while I was trying to get pregnant. After all that I (and especially John) had put up with for that time, it was insulting. Robert seemed to have no awareness of the sacrifices I had made in my normal life for him and Jean. Still, there was no point in getting angry about it now.

We had agreed that it was time for Jean and me to get to know each other better, and that was the top priority on my agenda.

Jean and I met on our own for the first time in April, at a teashop near Victoria Station. I was really surprised by her manner. Most of the time the conversation was just trite old chit-chat. We hardly talked about the pregnancy at all. Once she asked me if the baby was moving yet and when I said it was, she looked worried.

'But isn't it too early for it to be moving?'

I could tell that she was still worried about whether it was Robert's baby, but I wasn't going to argue. In as calm a voice as I could manage I tried to assuage her fears.

91

'I could feel my own babies moving very early on as well. It's not unusual, really it isn't.' She seemed satisfied with that answer for the moment, so I tried to get her to think more about the positive aspects of the whole thing.

'Would you like to be present at the birth?' I asked her. 'You're certainly welcome, as far as I'm concerned.'

She said she would, but that Robert wasn't too sure about the idea. 'He thinks it might look suspicious if we were both there.'

I didn't know what to think, really, because Robert had said on another occasion that he would like to be there at the birth to hold my hand. I had been very pleased when he said that, and I had said that it would be very nice if he did. The only problem was that he had said this to me when we were in bed together. I did feel disappointed that he had apparently changed his mind, but I didn't feel that I could repeat this conversation, considering the circumstances in which it took place. In any case, Jean said that it was still possible that he would come, so I decided not to think about it until the time came.

The next week we met again. I realised around this time that I hadn't spoken to Robert for weeks, and that made me feel very sad, after such close and intimate contact over so many months. I suppose he was deliberately drawing back now, letting Jean have her turn without him around.

I was still puzzled by her attitude. I didn't think she was sharing the pregnancy as much as she could or should. If I was in her position, I'd be pestering the girl non-stop about what was going on. I'd have wanted to know how the baby felt, whether it was kicking or moving, and would have been rushing out to buy things for the baby immediately.

But there was nothing like that coming from Jean, or very little. She did ask me once whether I thought it was a boy or a girl. Robert had once said that he thought it was a girl, and seemed to imply that I ought to think so too – that was his preference. I had told him that I actually thought it was a

92

boy, just as I instinctively thought that my own children were boys.

Jean was pleased when I told her what I thought – she wanted a boy. She said that she wanted to paint the baby's room blue and that Robert wanted to paint it pink. She had won.

Jean also said she wanted to learn to knit, so that she could make baby clothes. But that was one of the few things she said that suggested any real enthusiasm about the baby.

*   *   *

I met Robert and Jean every three weeks or so during these middle months. It was strange but they always seemed rather reluctant to put themselves out by coming over to my part of town for our meetings. They didn't flatly refuse, but there was something in the way they acted whenever the subject was raised. They'd say, 'Where shall we go then? Do you want us to come over to you?' If I said yes, they would come back with something like, 'Well, we don't finish work until late, and then with traffic we won't be able to get over to you before such and such a time.' Although they did usually come over to my side of town, I felt constantly as if I should have been going to theirs. Even when I was months pregnant they acted as if they were being put out, and occasionally I did agree to meet them halfway. I resented having to make the effort, particularly when it was very hot. Struggling along on the tube and trains when you're five or six months pregnant can be incredibly trying.

I did resent Robert and Jean at times like this. I still liked them but I felt very strongly that they didn't put nearly as much effort as I did into making things work. From the very first meeting I was always the one who brought up problems, and it stayed that way throughout. If I hadn't, Robert and Jean would have swept a lot of things under the carpet.

At times, when I reflected on what I was doing, I did find

myself wishing that the couple I had found to work with were more spontaneous than Robert and Jean. I would think, 'Well, here I am having a baby for someone else and I'm more excited about it than they are.' But then I would remind myself that everything could not be perfect. Life just didn't work out that way. I also knew that, after all, I am not perfect myself, and perhaps I was pushing them for emotions that they were not willing or able to display. I decided that I should think a lot more about how they were feeling and how bizarre it must have been for them. There was Jean, knowing that another woman was walking around with her husband's baby inside her, but that she, Jean, was going to be the recipient of that baby. Deep down I could understand the problems that this must have caused for her.

I was certainly having no problems being pregnant by then. I was loving it: the actual feeling of being pregnant was a joy. That's probably why I got those maternal feelings of wanting another baby of my own. I longed to be able to feel love for the baby, to chat to it as I chatted to my own boys when they were inside me. I would have loved to go to the shops and buy things for it. But I couldn't do that because it wasn't my own baby. I would have to wait for Jean before doing any of that.

None the less, I liked the fact that I was carrying around a baby inside me. That made all the little problems bearable and worthwhile. I had realised at the very beginning that things would not all go smoothly from beginning to end. My frustrations with Robert and Jean were only to be expected. But I did wish it were different, and I felt increasingly anxious about how they were going to think of me after the birth.

The feeling of being rejected by Robert was still particularly strong. It was a human reaction, I suppose, and perfectly natural. After having sex with the man and bearing his baby I thought that he should have felt more emotion towards me. But then I would think that it was a good job he

94

didn't, because something nasty could have happened: we might have fallen in love or something!

But even taking that into account, I still found that he was drawing back too much for my liking. He obviously felt the dangers of becoming too involved with me, but I thought he was taking things to the opposite extreme of coldness and lack of concern. What upset me most of all was the fact that I had originally explained to them the kind of intense relationship I wanted, but they continued to hold back as if everything might still come crashing down. Every mother-to-be has worries about her pregnancy but you can't let them surface and take over the whole pregnancy in the way that Robert and Jean were doing. You really can't spend the whole nine months worrying about what can go wrong and thinking that the worst things are bound to happen. You'd be a nervous wreck if you did.

Robert had still not decided about whether he was going to be at the birth. The third time I saw Jean she said he still hadn't made up his mind. I began to wonder how he would react to the birth if he did in fact witness it. It's such an emotional thing, and it would be *his* baby. Would the sight of all the pain I was going through make him realise that he was not getting such a bad deal after all? I wondered whether it would. He still complained about how much money it was costing him, and I felt that he had no appreciation of what he was getting for his money – and how tiny the sum was from my point of view. I believed he would decide to be there in the end, and I hoped he would be.

At this point, however, I was having doubts about how easy it would be to arrange for them both to be there. At our second meeting Jean asked me if, because of the story I'd given to the doctor, she would be able to be at the birth. Her question planted the seed of doubt in my mind, and I worried all the more because the way she asked the question suggested that she really did want to be there. Until then I hadn't been sure, but now I was.

95

I told Jean I didn't know, and hoped that I could explain it all to my doctor. I would have to tell her that my 'boyfriend's' wife and I had become very chummy during my pregnancy, and that she and her husband wanted to be present at the birth. I would say very emphatically that I didn't have any objections, and then just hope for the best. I thought I had a good chance, though I knew I'd have to gauge the doctor's attitude before knowing for certain whether I could ask the question.

Life was beginning to get complicated, as I was having to remember what I'd told different people about the pregnancy. My parents-in-law were already prepared for the loss of a third grandchild, while the neighbours thought I was having a normal pregnancy. I hadn't yet said anything was out of the ordinary. It was difficult keeping the two lots of stories straight.

This confusion nearly made me catch myself out one Sunday when a neighbour came round for tea with a mail-order catalogue for baby clothes. I had to go over it with her, commenting and checking prices and pretending that I might order some of the things listed.

Then, out of nowhere, my neighbour asked me, 'Where's the new one going to sleep?'

I was nonplussed. I simply hadn't thought about that at all, since I knew that the baby was never going to spend a single night in our house, and I didn't know what to say.

'Oh,' I finally replied, 'We're clearing out the box room. That will do for the time being, the baby can sleep there, and then, uh, we'll probably build an extension at the back of the house when it gets bigger.' I was so nervous, I thought she must see that I wasn't telling the truth.

She seemed satisfied, however, and if she suspected anything she certainly didn't let on. But then she asked me another awkward question.

'Are you looking forward to the baby now?'

This was tricky because I had previously told her that

John and I didn't want any more children, that in fact we had no intention whatsoever of having more. She had surely been surprised to hear that I was pregnant again, and I had pretended to be somewhat annoyed about the 'accident'. I got the impression that she had been waiting to ask this question for weeks.

So I had to acknowledge all that in my reply, in a way that didn't arouse her suspicions.

'Well, I am now,' I said. 'I can't say that I was at first, because it was such a surprise, and I wasn't planning for it or prepared for it. But now I've got used to the idea, I'm really very keen. I'm very happy about it, actually.'

We talked about names for the baby. I said I liked Jenny and Frank and Alan. I talked enough to seem interested but not so much that I might have looked nervous. I did feel at the time that she was a little bit suspicious but she probably wasn't at all. My mind had to work overtime to cope with the strain of keeping two stories going at once, and sometimes I got panicky about slipping up.

*   *   *

In May, when I was just over five months pregnant, I gave up my job as planned. I was sad to leave, as I had liked my boss and workmates, but there was no alternative. I had already told my boss that I didn't want to return after the baby was born because I wanted to stay at home and look after the children, so that was settled.

The day I left he gave me a huge bunch of roses and a kiss.

'You know you can always come back,' he told me. 'You're a great asset. Welcome back any time.'

Everyone else was very friendly as well. They had been very tolerant about my morning sickness and the time off I took to see the doctors, and I liked them all. By the time I left that day I was nearly in tears. Going home on the tube, I thought good and hard about what I was doing and why, about what

97

the most important things were in being a surrogate mother. I had gone into it because of the friendship I wanted with Robert and Jean, yet I had seen Jean only a few times up till then, and I felt there was something fundamental missing from the whole relationship. But I clung to the idea that, as the pregnancy progressed, it would get easier and we would all get closer. Deep down I felt confident that this would happen.

*   *   *

The one thing I feared about being a surrogate mother was that the social services might find out about me. I had nothing to hide, but I didn't want them nosing around in my life. I'm a very private person and hate the idea of someone watching me, inspecting me. Social workers are never any help, whatever they may think. All they ever do is want to find out the ins and outs of everything, and then they put you on their files; and once they've got you there, there's not a thing you can do about it. It's like the police having a file on you for some minor misdeed you may or may not have carried out as a teenager, and regardless of the circumstances that file is with you for life. I don't know what circumstances might make them haul out my social security child welfare files, but I'd hate to think what was in there.

My deepest fear has always been that, owing to my background, they might try to take my children away from me. This is probably irrational, but after the way I grew up I can't shake off the thought. And it came back stronger than ever after I started working with Robert and Jean. I'm not really frightened of people finding out who I am: I could cope with that, and even explain it to my in-laws and my neighbours if necessary. What did frighten me was the thought that the social services would get their hooks into me and come round to the house and assess me and my boys and make a big case out of us. Once they've got the hooks in, there's precious little you can do to get them out. I only did it

98

by virtually disappearing: my mother didn't know where I was living, and I just dropped out of the social services' sight. If they're still aware of my existence, they haven't shown it, and I want to keep things that way.

It was all this that made the secrecy and the careful planning so important. None of us could afford to make a mistake.

Whatever my disappointments with Robert and Jean, I never considered breaking my agreement with them. By the time I was five-and-a-half months pregnant, I didn't have much trouble feeling detached from the baby; I had finally persuaded myself that it wasn't my baby. While I knew I could walk away with it, I would never consider doing so. Robert and Jean trusted me, and I was not going to let them down. I knew it would be pretty difficult, handing the baby over to them, but I knew I would recover from this. Never for a minute did I worry that I would let them down. And I wouldn't let myself down, either, because this had become important for me too. I wanted to prove to them that any mistrust they might have felt was unjustified.

We had never discussed what would happen after the baby was born, whether I would see it or not. I think a part of me assumed that, because we were friends, I would get to see the baby later, whenever I came visiting at their house. Thinking on those lines, I had decided that I wouldn't want to see it too soon after leaving it with them. I planned to wait until it was two or three months old before I saw it again. When the baby was still a newborn I would be too close to it, but later, once Robert and Jean had established a relationship with the baby, my own closeness would have ended. And I would have done a lot of physical and emotional healing by then, so seeing the baby might be like seeing any friend's baby. I would look out of curiosity and interest, not because I thought to myself, 'That's *my* baby lying there.' That was the line of thought that I had to avoid at all costs.

I knew from an early stage that Robert was going to tell the child its origins when he thought it was old enough to understand, and I approved of that completely. I knew that I would be happy to see the child when it was eighteen or whatever, if indeed it wanted to meet me. I would explain why I had done what I had done, and would introduce him or her to my own boys, and hope that I could satisfy the child's curiosity about me. I hoped he or she wouldn't be disappointed, too.

I could understand the kind of curiosity that would lead a child to search out a mysterious parent like that. My father left when I was so young that I hardly knew him and didn't remember him at all after a few months. When I got older I became curious about him; I didn't have any idea of 'getting him back' or challenging him for having deserted us, I just wanted to meet him and know what sort of man he was, so I did track him down and saw him a couple of times. I found that I didn't really like him all that much as a person. The important thing was that I had satisfied my curiosity about him and, having done that, I didn't really see the need to continue to meet when all I accomplished was to deepen his sense of guilt about deserting us. But I would have been sorry never to have met him, and expected that the child I had for Robert and Jean was likely to feel the same way about me.

Whenever I analysed what was going on with Robert and Jean, I always came back to the fact that I was still dissatisfied with our friendship. There was just no closeness there. We knew each other pretty well, so we were friends in that sense, but there was still something important missing.

I think that what was missing was mainly trust. We were tied together, it seemed, mostly by the business arrangement we had. They still seemed to think of me as someone who was doing something for them on a commercial basis, for a fee, and they were worried that I was going to renege on my side of the bargain. That was the main sensation I got from them. Personal trust, personal feeling, seemed to be given only reluctantly. I felt that I was actually trusting them a lot more

100

than they were trusting me. After all, I was going to hand over their baby long before I got all the money they had said they would give me. Perhaps in their heart of hearts they didn't believe I would hand over the baby when the time came.

Things improved a little bit when we met for dinner in May. I talked to them about the baby, and for once they seemed to appreciate what I was saying. For instance, I told them it was kicking well, and that I'd been chatting to it, telling it about its parents. There was a slight flicker of a smile on Robert's face when I said that.

'Only good things, I hope?'

'Oh yes,' I replied. 'I've been telling it that you're interested in boats, that it's going to have a real sailor for a daddy, so it will have to get used to life on the ocean waves.' They both laughed at that, and I was really pleased to see them at last displaying some spontaneous emotion!

Now that things had lightened up a little, I took the opportunity to ask them when they were going to stop being so cautious.

'It's six whole months now, and there's very little chance that anything is going to go wrong. Of course, something *can* still go wrong, but that's just a chance that every parent-to-be has to accept. You should try to relax a little, to enjoy it more.'

I couldn't tell if they were listening to me seriously, but they seemed to take in what I had said. At least I had said it, and maybe I had begun to get across to them that with so many other problems to think about, they should stop inventing new ones to complicate matters even more. I hoped it had sunk in.

*　　*　　*

I was enjoying being back at home, a non-working mother looking after the dozens of little household chores. Doing this had brought John and me even closer together, and I could see now that my earlier maternal feelings had subsided. This was not a coincidence, I am sure.

I was glad the urge to have another baby had almost completely disappeared. Though I wouldn't really call it an urge. I didn't feel different from any married woman who gets a little upset when her kids are getting older and more independent. Every mother goes through this phase. You get used to these little humans being utterly dependent on you for everything, even affection; then they start having their own friends and don't need quite so much attention, and you begin to feel somewhat redundant as a mother. Especially as they start growing into children rather than toddlers. You see that they're on the way to real independence, and that's a frightening moment – at least it is for most of the women I know, myself included. When you get frightened you start to think that maybe you want another one, someone else who'll be dependent on you like that. I think that a lot of the so-called accidents women have – unexpectedly getting pregnant again when their children are starting to drift away – are anything but accidents. They're a little insurance policy, a guarantee that they'll still have someone to look after.

I'm a little too aware of why I do things to let that happen to me, though I can certainly understand how it happens to other women. When I find myself thinking about another baby, I analyse why and sometimes the reasons are not good enough to make it worth committing myself for five years to another dependent bundle. You have to weigh that against the things you're passing up, like the chance to go abroad with your other children.

I've always thought hard about things, ever since I had to puzzle out why I didn't have a father and why my mother was the way she was. The habit has stayed with me: I think about why I'm doing what I'm doing and what I want out of life, and then I go out and try to get it.

My first aim is always self-preservation, and I try to achieve that with whatever means are necessary. I'm not much of a feminist, I suppose: I'm for myself as an individual, not for women as part of society. I don't let anyone mess me around because I'm a woman, but neither do I remind them of it constantly. I just try to do what I want. Of course I take my family into account, and look after the usual domestic chores. But I'm not one of those women who cheerily let their lives revolve around the washing. I do as much of those things as needs doing to keep the place reasonably clean and tidy, and to keep us all well fed. But if I fancy taking the children swimming before the cleaning is done, I take them. My housework is done when I've got nothing better to do, not the other way around. My neighbours think I'm a bit funny, but I don't care.

* * *

When I was due to go for my hospital appointment in the sixth month, Jean surprised me by ringing and asking if she could come too. I was very pleased, and told her that of course she could. We arranged to meet outside the clinic fifteen minutes before the time of my appointment.

Jean was right on time, and I could see she was quite excited. When we went in together, I told the nurse she was my sister-in-law and asked if she could sit in with me. That was all right with the nurse, so Jean was there with me the whole time except when I was being physically examined.

Since we were there, I asked the doctor if I could have an ultrasound scan. She said I didn't need one because I was all right, but when I said I really wanted one she agreed. I had insisted for Jean's sake, though of course I didn't tell the doctor this.

While we were waiting to go into the ultrasound room, the baby started moving. 'Give me your hand – quick,' I said to Jean. I put her hand on one side of my stomach and prodded

103

the baby on the other side, and it obligingly kicked in the direction of Jean. She looked amazed.

When I went in for the ultrasound, Jean sat next to me. It was a portable monitor rather than a high overhead type. I couldn't see much over the nurse's arm but Jean had an excellent view, and she was riveted to the screen the whole way through. The nurse pointed out to her the baby's arms and legs and spinal column, and gave us several good views of the face, in which we could see clearly the eyes, nose and mouth.

One thing we couldn't see was the sex, as the nurse ran the monitor rather quickly over the legs. I didn't mind that: I think it's more fun not to know, and Jean agreed.

Afterwards we had coffee and she seemed more animated than at any other time before this. I think seeing the baby on the ultrasound screen had suddenly made her wake up to the reality of it. She asked me many more questions about how it felt and I was happy to tell her everything I could.

And Jean herself talked on and on. The baby's room was all decorated, she told me, and she was planning to start buying things for it soon. I said that if she wanted any advice about nappies and formula feed and all that, I was very happy to give her a few tips. I was a bit surprised that she didn't take me up on the offer then. She just fell silent and looked down at her feet.

Ah well, I thought to myself. Two steps forward and one step back. When are they ever going to relax?

CHAPTER EIGHT

Late June to Late August

As I LAY in bed one morning in early July, thinking about getting up to make the boys' breakfast, it suddenly occurred to me that I ought to write a book about what I was doing. Deep down, like most people I suppose, I have always had a yearning to write a book. I used to think that I would write something about my childhood, a novel or personal memoirs. But there were always other things to do and I had no compelling reason to write, so those thoughts had remained pure fantasy.

Now I had a very good reason – lots of them, in fact. One would be to put forward the case for surrogate motherhood, to show that it is not necessarily a bad thing. It might provide me with a bit of welcome income, and I certainly wasn't going to complain about that. And perhaps most important, writing would give me something to focus on after the baby was born. A book would be something I created myself, my replacement 'baby' perhaps; it would make up in part for the other baby that I would not have.

The more I thought about it, the more I liked the idea. When I mentioned it to John, he agreed that it was a good idea but had certain reservations.

'What about Robert and Jean?' he asked.

'What about them?' I replied.

'Well, I don't think they would be too pleased, would they?'

I hadn't thought of that, but didn't really see the problem. 'It'll be anonymous,' I told him. 'No one would ever connect them with the book. I could disguise everyone, make all the details different so no one would recognise any of the... characters, I suppose you could call them.'

John looked doubtful. 'I think you'd better discuss it with them first,' he cautioned. 'After all, you don't want them suing you or anything.'

I nodded in agreement, knowing he was right. I would have to discuss it with Robert and Jean. It was only fair, really, if I was going to put them in the book as 'characters'.

Still, I was worried about what would happen when I did raise the issue. I hadn't seen either of them since my visit to the hospital with Jean, and we had spoken on the phone only very occasionally. The circumstances were hardly ideal for springing something like this book idea on them. But I knew it had to be done, so I planned to talk to Jean about it the next time we met.

We hadn't planned to meet again for almost another two weeks, so I thought it wouldn't hurt to do a little groundwork on the idea of writing a book. I knew I'd need a publisher, and thought that I'd better find out how to go about getting one. My friend Carol was back from Germany for a two-week holiday and I knew that her husband knew people in the publishing world, so I got in touch with her.

Carol's first response was typical: 'Will I be in it?' But she was genuinely enthusiastic about the idea, and she proved to be very helpful. They did indeed know someone who worked in publishing – not for a publishing house but for a literary agent – and she said she would get in touch with him for me.

After that, it all happened so fast. A few phone calls were made, and within days I found myself sitting across the desk from Carol's agent friend, talking nonstop about myself and what I was doing. The agent was very interested in my story, and thought that it would probably make a good book. He felt pretty certain that if I could work up an outline for it, he could find a publisher. The agent was also completely sympathetic about the need for secrecy. We discussed how I would keep my identity secret and not pose any threat to Robert or Jean – or, especially, the baby. I liked the agent, too, even though I didn't know the first thing about his business.

By the end of the week I was sitting down and planning an outline. It was very exciting to me – a completely new and unexpected adventure. I could hardly believe my luck.

In those first days I went through something that I'm told affects many first-time authors. With the vision of huge book sales, movie rights, paperback rights and all the other things the agent mentioned dancing before me, I saw visions of thousands of pounds dropping into my lap by magic. I don't know how long it takes other beginners to see the folly of that line of thought, but it certainly didn't take me long. I quickly realised that there was a lot of hard work to be done before even a penny showed its face, and plenty of waiting to do when the work was over. The few people who make piles of money from writing are the lucky ones, and there's nothing easy about it.

*   *   *

John and I had continued to get on very well and the idea of the book gave us a lot to talk about now, like a brand-new hobby. It also gave us a new way of talking more about the pregnancy, in which John continued not to show much interest. He rarely mentioned Jean and Robert, though he did often joke about my pregnant state. 'Here comes waddle,' he would say when I walked into a room. He didn't actually seem to take this pregnancy any differently from those of our own children. With them he hadn't wanted to feel my stomach so he could feel the baby move or anything like that, and he was true to form this time too. He just made his little jokes about my figure and left it at that.

107

Now and again the children said something, however.

'When's the baby coming out?' they would ask me.

'Not yet,' I'd reply. 'It won't be for a long time yet.'

And that would be it. To them it seemed like such a long time that I had been pregnant, it became less and less a novelty all the time. When it came to it, I knew, they would ask questions for a couple of days, or weeks, and then forget all about it.

In July, the subject of surrogate motherhood was very much in the news again when the Warnock Committee published its report. By that time I couldn't be bothered to read much about it. This was a sharp contrast to the early days, when I bought any magazine or newspaper that announced a story on the subject and watched every television programme on the subject as well. Now I tended only to select the bits and pieces that sounded sympathetic. Anything that sounded hostile I couldn't bring myself to read.

I did see snatches about the Warnock Committee on television, however, and heard Mary Warnock (as she was then) say that she thought all surrogate motherhood should be illegal. Maybe she knew that there was no way she could stop people like me from doing it, but apparently she wanted to make it as difficult as possible for doctors, to make them suffer if they tried to help. If we had the baby without a doctor's participation we would be committing a crime, and now the doctors would also be acting criminally if they helped in a surrogate pregnancy. By taking away medical support she was effectively trying to put an end to the whole activity, since we had to have the doctor there – barring an act of God – when the baby was born.

Legislation wouldn't affect me personally, but I knew that it would affect people trying to do the same thing, and that bothered me. Personally I don't think there should be any private surrogate mothering agencies: they are middlemen exploiting both parties. I would rather see the government

108

set up surrogate centres, which would introduce childless couples to willing surrogates as part of the NHS. A kind of 'Dateline'. It would be non-profit-making that way. A minimal charge paid by the parents could cover the paperwork and administration, and everyone would be guaranteed adequate medical care. I don't believe that women should be able to do surrogate mothering as a 'profession', since that would encourage those who see it solely as a way of making money and haven't thought of the emotional aspects at all.

There are problems even with the NHS centre idea. It would undoubtedly involve a lot of screening and selecting by medical and psychological tests. Not only does that not necessarily work, it also lengthens the whole process. And people would undoubtedly be rejected. As a matter of fact, there's a good chance that I would have been rejected myself. My background, and the fact that I had been depressed sometimes in the past, would not look very good to whoever did the screening. And Jean might not come out looking too great either. The very fact that she had such a hard time when she couldn't have children might make them reject her! You never can tell.

Anyway, the publication of the Warnock Report gave me much more to think about while I was planning an outline for the agent. He rang me up the day after the report came out to see how it was going – casually mentioning, with badly concealed excitement, that the report certainly did not hurt our chances of selling the book. The thought had occurred to me, too.

But I still had the problem of broaching the subject with Robert and Jean. With our relationship so shaky, I was frightened by the idea of it. I rang Jean shortly after my visit to the literary agent and asked if she would like to go shopping with me at Mothercare.

I was going to go shopping there anyway. The neighbours had started asking whether I had bought anything, and this made me realise that I had to buy some baby things to take back to my house. I had borrowed some stuff from Linda, and she also knitted me some cardigans which I would simply give back to her afterwards. (She would use them later for her children's dolls.) But I needed to do some shopping so that it would seem as if I was preparing properly for the arrival of a new baby. I thought I might combine that with a chance to talk to Jean.

Jean sounded pleased at the idea, and we arranged to meet at the Mothercare in Oxford Street the following Wednesday.

I was delighted. I'd been dying to go shopping with her all along. I always think that one of the best ways for two women to be friendly is to go shopping together, and pop into the pub midway for a drink and so on. It's much better to be staggering along the road with bags of shopping and be dying for a drink together than to meet on a formal basis over dinner. It seemed as if we might start getting along on just that basis now.

We met outside Mothercare the following Wednesday at 3 p.m. and walked around for a while. Jean didn't buy very much – or not as much as I'd have bought, anyway. I'm the sort of person who buys an armful of clothes; Jean was buying one of this and one of that. She got a couple of little vests, a nightie, a little top-and-tail bowl for washing in, little pants, some babygro's. Just a few bits and bobs really. She didn't get anything fancy, no suits or big things like prams or cots. They were planning to get those later on, probably at the last minute. Of course, she was in an unusual position in that she *could* get them at the last minute. An ordinary mother would have been too busy with everything else.

We discussed the merits of one pram over another, and Jean did want to know my opinion about which was better and so forth. But when I suggested one she tended to just hum and haw about it, so I moved on to something else. I didn't want her to feel that she was being pushed into buying any particular item. She didn't pay as much attention as I would have to the fancy bits and pieces, just concentrated on the practical things. I would have been grabbing frilly bootees and maybe a little matinee jacket they had, but Jean was having none of that. And everything she bought was white. Apparently Robert doesn't like yellow, and she didn't want to buy pink or blue, so that really only left her with one choice – white. Not a colour I would have chosen, but there we were.

As we went round the shop together, it never really bothered me that she was doing the buying and I wasn't. I didn't feel any pangs of regret that I wasn't buying baby clothes for a baby that I'd be keeping myself. I did feel, though, that I'd have bought more of the pretty things. For instance there was a little cot with a canopy over it like a four-poster bed. I thought to myself, 'If I had another baby I'd love to have one of those for it.' I liked admiring the things that were there. And I felt like an experienced shopper for baby items. But I didn't resent the fact that Jean was doing the buying.

It was actually great fun, because there are many more really nice things around than when I had my two boys – things that are both nice to look at and much more practical. Like the new prams. When I had my first I went out and bought the best and most expensive, a huge great Silver Cross. Now I wouldn't touch one with a barge-pole. They're so big and unwieldy you can't manoeuvre them round doors or anything. I told Jean about this problem, and pointed out all the modern buggies, especially the lie-back type which is like a triangle. I thought that was really great and practical, but Jean preferred this little corduroy carrycot on wheels. I also liked the slings that enable you to hold the baby to you, but Jean didn't agree at all. She seemed to think the baby would be hanging out of it or having its head lolling about. Of course, that's not true if you use them properly. I'd certainly use one when I went shopping with a tiny baby, but Jean didn't like it.

Jean was going to buy a plastic-covered changing mat,

111

and I told her that you could now get a new type which folds up with a zip and turns into a bag you can use for carrying the baby's things around. When you're going out – to a friend's house or whatever – you can unzip the bag, take the stuff out, change the baby on the bag, and then fold it all back up again. She liked the idea, but the only ones they had there were cheap and nasty. I told her she'd be able to get better than that. Then we looked at the different milks you can buy and the different bottles. She was going to get a steriliser with four large heavy glass bottles in it, but I told her there were much lighter ones with plastic bottles which are easier to clean.

We enjoyed doing all this shopping. Halfway through we stopped for a cup of tea and saw a woman with a week-old baby in the restaurant, and chatted merrily about that for a few minutes.

Then, with my heart racing a little bit, I finally managed to raise the subject of the book. I thought it would be best to try the idea out on her alone, before telling Robert about it. Since Jean was being so friendly, I decided that this was a good time.

'Um, you know, I've been thinking seriously about writing a book about all this,' I said.

She looked a bit shocked, and I quickly tried to alleviate her fears about it.

'Anonymously, of course. It would be our story, but with all the names and details changed. I wouldn't want anyone to know who I was, and I certainly wouldn't want them to find out who you were either.'

'Oh, I see...' She seemed a little doubtful still, but her main fear was relieved.

'No, we both have our families to think of,' I added.

'Yes, of course. Well, as long as everything is secret, then that's fine as far as I'm concerned.' Jean really didn't seem to mind. She agreed with me when I said I wanted to write the book to show that surrogate mothering wasn't a bad thing, and that it could be done without the whole world knowing about it or commercial agencies or lawyers being involved. She approved of that completely, and I was very pleased.

But it hadn't been Jean's reaction that I was worried about: it was Robert's. After the way he had gone on so much about money, about the sacrifice they were making and the need to economise, he might be peeved that I was making money from a book in addition to what I was getting from them. It occurred to me that he might even be peeved enough to blow the whistle on me. I sounded out Jean on this as tactfully as I could, and she wasn't concerned about it at all.

'Oh no,' she said immediately. 'Robert wouldn't even consider doing that. Even if he wanted to, he couldn't do it without also revealing our identity, and that's the last thing in the world he wants. He would destroy our lives as well as yours.'

Jean was so adamant about this that I couldn't help being convinced by her. Although she's a more passive partner in their marriage than Robert, I don't think he would risk upsetting her whatever he wanted to do to me. They were prepared to be honest to their family, but they certainly didn't want the whole world to know.

That made me feel a lot better. And Jean said she wouldn't tell Robert about it, though I knew full well she would. But that was all right. He'd be finding out soon enough anyway.

After leaving Mothercare we went to John Lewis and were still looking round when it started to shut. The time had passed so quickly, neither of us had had any idea of how late it was.

By that time we had a huge Mothercare bag and a smaller bag with a few odds and ends. Jean paid for it, but I took the big bag home with me. It seemed strange, shopping that way for a baby which was inside me but would later be transferred – like the clothes and things we had bought – to Jean. She took home the John Lewis bag and said she'd be over for the rest when the baby's room was sorted out.

113

I went home feeling very happy. It had been a great day, not quite like two ordinary friends shopping as they normally would but as near to that as you can get in an all-of-a-sudden friendship.

I was also glad that it was Jean who actually suggested that we make a date for all of us to have dinner together the next week. I was very pleased, as I wanted to have dinner with them but didn't feel, with the way things were at that time, that I could mention it myself – particularly as I was a bit fed up with taking the initiative. But I was most relieved by what she had said about the book.

The next day, Robert rang. Jean had told him about the book, as I knew she would; and he was upset, as I knew he would be. He asked me to consider what I was doing very carefully.

'There's not much I can do to stop you, obviously, but I must ask you to change your mind about it, Kirsty. It just makes the entire venture much riskier. It will lay all of us open to exposure – much more open than we would be otherwise. I really think that it would be a mistake.'

'Yes,' I thought, 'thanks to me we haven't come across any major hitches and all the loose ends have been tied up.' But all I said was 'I really want to do it, Robert.' My voice was very firm, and I could tell that he knew I meant business. There was nothing he could do to stop me.

After that not a lot was said about the book. In fact, the book was never mentioned again, and this fact helped me get on with it.

Our dinner date for the following week was still on, anyway. As I was getting ready to go, John said something completely unexpected.

'I want to go with you,' he announced. I was buttoning my blouse, and I stopped for a moment. Until this time he had never expressed any interest in meeting Robert and Jean, and had only talked to them briefly on the phone. I was actually quite pleased that he was expressing this interest now, and

114

didn't mean to put him off at all, but I was so surprised that I hesitated for a moment.

He misinterpreted my hesitation.

'What's wrong?' he quickly asked. 'Don't you want me to come?'

'Oh no,' I replied. 'You can come if you like. I don't mind at all.'

I meant that, but I did worry about him a little bit. He is very passive, not a fireball like me, and I was worried that Robert might try to put him down. I felt protective towards him.

But I could easily understand why he wanted to come. He was curious about what they looked like, these people I'd been spending time with and talking about. I'd never gone into details about them, and he wanted to see for himself what they were like.

It occurred to me that perhaps I should ring Robert and Jean to say that John was going to be coming along, but then I decided it would be better just to turn up. John got me to wait a few minutes while he shaved, combed his hair, and put on a smart shirt and pair of trousers. He was obviously out to impress!

On the way to the restaurant I warned John that Robert could be a domineering sort sometimes, and that he could be sarcastic if he felt like it. So John wasn't to be upset by him. At the same time I told John that he shouldn't start on Robert either, it would only get him going. John seemed to understand that, but he was still determined to come with me.

So we turned up at dinner together, John and me. We arrived at the restaurant first, and sat down at the table Robert had booked. When he and Jean arrived and approached the table, they were quite shocked to see John. They just stood there in silence for a moment. Then Robert, to his credit, stuck his hand out.

'Ah ha,' he said. 'So we meet the elusive John.'

John shook Robert's hand, said hello, and Robert and Jean sat down. I thought the ice had broken pretty easily.

The evening went well. John and Robert asked each other a lot of questions, about what kind of music they liked, that sort of thing – nothing about surrogate mothers or what I was doing for Robert and Jean or anything like that. Robert was really sizing up John and John was doing the same.

And Jean was in better form this time than she had been at some of our earlier meetings. Following our shopping trip together, she seemed more relaxed and took more interest in the baby than was usual for her. She and Robert both asked how it was and looked to see how big I was every time I got up from the table.

After the meal, as we were walking down the road to our car, everyone was in a very good mood. I said it just so happened that the baby had decided not to move that evening. Robert said I should let him know when it changed its mind so they could all start groping my stomach. He said Jean wanted to have a feel, too.

I was amazed by this sudden upsurge of interest on their part, but perhaps they were simply feeling more relaxed now. It had come rather later than I would have hoped, but it made me happy none the less.

As John and I drove home I asked him whether it had crossed his mind, when he saw Robert, that that was the man I'd had sex with – the only other man apart from John himself. He said it had.

'But that doesn't bother me too much. I don't hate him for it or anything,' he added.

I asked John what he thought of Robert and he said he thought he was all right. He could also, however, see exactly what I meant when I said he was domineering.

That obviously made the sex part of it easier for John: he knew that Robert didn't have the sort of personality I could get on with for very long. I think John realised that night that Robert wasn't a threat to him in any way. His curiosity

116

was satisified. And he had liked Jean, who he said was a nice person.

*　　*　　*

I had started keeping notes for my book, but I had to be very careful about hiding everything away when any of the neighbours came round. An amusing if somewhat alarming incident occurred in August when a Scottish woman was in the news because she had had a baby for an infertile couple. That night, one of the neighbours came round and brought her sister with her. It was quite late in the evening and we were all sitting around and having tea and chatting. I was griping a little bit to the neighbour's sister about my baby being an accident, and she said all of a sudden, 'You ought to do one of those surrogate mother things.'

My heart skipped a beat and I felt my face go red.

'What?' I demanded to know in a shrill voice. But the day was saved because my neighbour hadn't heard of surrogate mothers at all, and she innocently asked, 'What's that?'

'Oh, you must have heard of it,' I replied a little more calmly. 'It's been all over the papers and television this morning. It's a woman who gives birth to a baby and then gives it away. I think some of them get paid for it – I think that's what it's all about.' And her sister chimed in with, 'They get lots and lots of money for it!'

'Ooh,' I laughed, 'do they? That's interesting!' And we all made a big joke of it, saying that every one of our friends should go out and get pregnant immediately and give the baby to someone for money. I changed the subject at the first opportunity. I thought at the time that if they both knew what was really involved in these cases, they wouldn't treat the matter so lightly – all they could think about was the money changing hands.

What did impress me about their reaction was that they didn't pass judgement immediately. They didn't say that

117

surrogate mothers were horrible or wicked or anything like that. Still, I certainly wasn't ready to confide in them, or sorry that I hadn't owned up from the beginning. I was just glad I hadn't gone all funny when the subject came up. If I had blushed visibly, they certainly hadn't noticed it.

Still, close calls like that I was very happy to do without. After they had left, I rushed in to where John was reading and told him the whole thing. He laughed about it and so did I. But I wondered how many more times this sort of thing was going to happen before my nine months were finally up.

CHAPTER NINE

The Birth

AT FIVE O'CLOCK one Thursday morning in early September, five days before the baby was supposedly due, I woke up with a pain in my lower abdomen, deep below the bulge.

At first I thought my bladder was full so I went to the loo, but when I had finished the pain was still there. I lay in bed waiting, wondering what was going on. The pain waned somewhat but never went away, and after a while I started to get suspicious. Was this the beginning of labour? They do say that each one is different, even for the same woman, and this one might simply be a new kind for me. When the pain kept on for a while, my suspicion became a certainty. I shook John.

'Wake up,' I said. 'I think this is it.'

John groaned and rolled over again.

'Oh it can't be,' he mumbled through the pillow. 'It's too early. Go to sleep.' As he happily tried to do the same, I shook him again.

'No, this is definitely it. I'm sure of it... Wake up!'

No one ever got up more reluctantly than John did. He seemed unwilling even to open his eyes as he staggered out of bed and pulled on a bathrobe, then went downstairs to make a cup of tea. Meanwhile, I had a look for obvious signs that labour had begun. There was no spotting, so my waters couldn't have broken, but I knew, nonetheless, that labour was starting. It was just a matter of time now.

I felt quite nervous, since my own babies had had very quick, relatively easy births – the second birth happened within ninety minutes of onset of labour. I knew that this one would be just as quick if not quicker, and I needed forty minutes to get to the hospital!

The pain wasn't getting any worse, but neither was it getting any better. It was just more obvious. I knew I'd better get to the hospital. I focused all my thoughts on that.

As the pains grew stronger I consoled myself by thinking that if I really had started labour then it would all be over soon – probably by lunchtime. Today was definitely the day! It suddenly seemed hard to believe that this was all going to be over soon.

Then the strangeness of it all weighed in on me. I had already packed my bags for the hospital stay, as any expectant mother does, but had packed extra things for my stay with Robert and Jean: I wouldn't be coming home for quite some time. So the bag was enormous, and stuffed full. It would be very strange, I knew, to be going to their house afterwards rather than back to my own. It was also strange that I would be going to the hospital alone. John and I had agreed that there was no point in his coming too, and someone had to look after the children. But he had come along for my other two births, and it would be strange doing things differently this time.

Pretty soon I didn't have much energy for thinking about that or anything else – except the pains. They were getting worse. I phoned a cab and waited by the door. It arrived in about fifteen minutes.

John stood there with me in silence until we saw the cab pull up outside the door.

'Well, Kirsty, this is it.' And he gave me a hug and a kiss. 'I'll miss you,' he added.

'I'll miss you too,' I replied. And it certainly was true. We were not going to be seeing each other for ten or eleven days, and those would probably be pretty difficult days for me.

'I'll phone you as soon as I can,' I said.

'Fine. Please do.'

And that was it. I walked out the door and got into the cab.

*   *   *

When I gave the driver the name of the hospital, he glanced at my bulge and his eyes widened.

'You're not, are you?' he said.

'Well, yes, I am as a matter of fact. But don't worry about it. It's not an emergency. It'll be hours yet.'

'Are you sure about that?' he asked.

'Sure I'm sure,' I told him. 'This is my third time round.'

But he got nervous, and he drove like a maniac. All the way to the hospital I tried to calm him down, making jokes about anything I could think of. I said that my husband had to be at work so he couldn't come with me to the hospital, and anyway he'd seen our other children being born and had been sick in the waiting room. 'So he told me he'd sit this one out and wait for the reports,' I said. None of it was true, of course, but I was saying anything that came into my head. I asked the driver questions about his own children, and he said that he had watched them being born and wasn't going to have that going on in his cab.

'Oh, don't worry,' I reassured him. 'We've got hours yet.' I did my best to persuade him that he wasn't the only one who didn't want to see his cab turned into a labour ward.

It didn't do any good. He was too nervous. I got that way myself when he almost ran out of petrol while we were still a long way from the hospital, and had to find a petrol station to fill up. My pains were getting steadily worse, though of course I didn't tell him that. He had enough on his mind. There I was having regular pains and I was actually worried about making life difficult for the cabbie!

By the time we finally got to the hospital, I was all right

121

but the cabbie was a bit of a nervous wreck. They ushered me straight into an examination room.

The midwife was a friendly woman in her mid-thirties. She saw my big suitcase and I told her, in embarrassment, that I had brought my stuff with me. She knew that I was only booked in for forty-eight hours, yet here I was carrying what looked like enough clothes for a three-week holiday. She couldn't have known that I wouldn't be going home afterwards, and she must have thought I was pretty peculiar.

The midwife asked if I was sure that I had begun labour. I said that I couldn't be 100 per cent sure because it was so different from my first two, but I was pretty sure. She said they would give me an internal examination and see how it was going.

Just as she was about to give me the examination, a particularly bad pain came. I said she'd have to hang on a minute. When she did the examination finally she felt around my uterus and said I was definitely contracting. The cervical dilation required for delivery is ten centimetres and I had already dilated six – over halfway there. She told me that, and said that I'd have to go straight up to the labour ward. I couldn't delay for another minute.

I got up, very gently, and walked as slowly as I could to the lift. They put my stuff on a trolley, and we all got into the lift when it arrived.

As we were going up in the lift I realised that I still hadn't spoken to Robert and Jean. I hadn't bothered to phone them from home because I thought there was always the off-chance that it was a false alarm, and I didn't want them to get worried or disappointed about nothing. Now that the midwife had confirmed that labour was starting, I wanted to get hold of them.

When we got out of the lift and started walking to the labour ward, I kept searching for a public telephone but couldn't see one. Luckily, there was one in the labour ward, and whilst they were preparing everything I asked if it would be all right if I made a quick call. I told them that my husband was away, and that my brother and sister-in-law were going to see me through the delivery. The midwife seemed pleased.

'That's fine. Go on then, phone them.'

I dialled their number with my hands slightly trembling. I prayed that they would be in. It was about 8 a.m.

Robert answered after the third ring.

'Hello,' I said. 'It's me.'

'Hello, is everything all right?'

'Well, yes, but the doctors miscalculated a little bit. This is it. Today. It's happening today.'

Robert gasped. 'No, really!' he said. Then there was silence on the other end of the line, but I could tell he was smiling. When he spoke, I could tell he was smiling still.

'Jean was just saying that she wished it would be born today,' he said. 'Just five minutes ago she said that.'

'Well,' I replied, 'she's got her wish, but if you want to catch any of the action you'd better be quick about getting here.'

'Really? Do you think so?'

'I *know* so!' I replied. 'The labour ward is being prepared right now.'

'What! You mean you're actually at the hospital already? Good God, why didn't you let us know earlier?'

I explained that I hadn't wanted to upset them un-necessarily, and thought it best to wait. I hadn't realised it would happen so fast. But now I had been examined and I was already halfway there, so he'd better get a move on.

Robert was breathless.

'Jean's already in the shower. She'll be ready in no time. I've got to go to work for a while to look after a few things, but I'll be there afterwards.'

'All right,' I said. 'I've got to go now.' And we both hung up. I knew that Robert wouldn't be there on time.

After I hung up, the nurse approached and said she wanted

123

to break the waters so that they could attach the monitors.

That worried me: if they broke the waters now, things would be speeded up so much that Jean would never have the chance to arrive on time.

'Could you wait a little while? My sister-in-law hasn't arrived yet, and I would very much like her to be here because she wants to watch the birth. She only lives up the road.'

The midwife looked a little bit doubtful.

'Well, we don't want to hold things up too long,' she said.

'Oh, my other babies were born very fast. If they're anything to go by, we won't have long to wait at all.' So the midwife agreed to wait.

Jean arrived about a half-hour later, at 8.45 a.m. or so. She walked into the room, came straight over to me and said, 'Give us a kiss then.' I gave her a kiss. I was very happy to see her. We smiled broadly at each other and just watched the midwives get on with their bits and pieces.

A doctor, a young man, came in after a few minutes. He talked to the midwives for a few moments and then turned to me.

'I'll be back in a few hours to see how you're getting on,' he said.

'You'll be lucky,' I grinned.

He looked taken aback, so I explained what I meant.

'I shall deliver this baby within an hour,' I told him. 'You come back in a few hours and you'll miss the whole show.'

He nodded knowingly and muttered something like 'We'll see.' And then he was off. I knew what was going to happen but they didn't believe me; they never have done, since I'm not an expert as far as they're concerned.

I was surprised by Jean's reactions to everything. I had expected her to be flustered and nervous, but she was cool as a cucumber all through everything.

Over the next half-hour we concentrated on the contractions. They were very strong now and I needed to use the gas and air. I shed a few tears at this point, though not so

124

much from pain as from fear of the pain. The pain was pretty bad, however, as the contractions grew. I sweated but I was able to cope.

At about 9.30 a.m. the contractions began to get very, very painful. I started getting worried because I wasn't sure how much longer I would have to go on. It was the third stage of labour and the contractions were really bad. Having already had two babies, I knew what to expect, and it was not very pleasant at all.

Jean was great. She held my hand, and she was very cool about everything.

'Are you all right? Can I do anything?' she asked.

'No, I'm all right,' I told her. 'It's just that I know what's coming!'

Jean kept holding my hand and watching. She showed no signs of wanting to run for the door, or faint. If she felt that way, she hid her feelings well. I had expected her to be at least a little bit bothered, since it was the first time she had witnessed any birth, let alone that of a baby that was hers.

We kept exchanging glances whenever one of the midwives said anything to me about 'your baby', but of course neither of us did or said anything that would have given the game away.

Suddenly the big, excruciating pains hit. There is no way to describe these pains. I sort of yelled at the nurse to give me some drugs. In both my other births I had got through without them, but right towards the end I had wanted them and called for them. Of course, the midwives know that you are likely to call for them, and that the pain is very bad, but they have this subtle way of persuading you not to have them. They don't actually refuse, but in the meantime the baby is being born.

The time when I was crying for the drugs was the only part of it that seemed really difficult for Jean. She was simply concerned for me, and couldn't understand why I wasn't being given drugs when I was obviously in so much pain.

'Can't you even give her half a dose?' she asked the midwives. 'Can't she have anything? How much longer has she got to go through this?' She wasn't so much butting in as trying to help me. She thought they weren't taking enough notice of me.

I was very touched by Jean's concern. If I had been her, I'd have been paying much more attention to what was going on between the legs of the woman giving birth than to anything else in the world. The head was just about there, and delivery was imminent, and she was trying to get drugs for me. I'd have simply been waiting for the moment when that face would appear. But Jean was more concerned about my pain.

At 9.45 a.m. exactly, the baby was born. 'It's a little boy,' the nurse said. I couldn't see him. All I could see was the steam rising from his body.

It happened so fast and so suddenly I think everyone was surprised. The official timing of the labour was put down as one minute precisely, though it seemed like much longer to me. The timing starts with the appearance of the head and ends with the delivery, and that had all happened very fast.

In fact, it was a bit of a 'shock birth' because he came too fast. The midwives didn't have a chance to control the speed of the delivery, and that is traumatic for the woman's body and for the baby to a certain extent. But everything was okay.

I couldn't see the baby when it was between my legs. You never can, really, and with my own two boys I found this incredibly frustrating. I had immediately started twisting about trying to get a look. 'What is it, what is it?' I would ask. I wanted to see them the minute they came out of me, and before they had been cleaned up. The first time the baby was shown to me only when it had been cleaned and wrapped up. With my second, I had insisted that it be delivered onto my stomach and my breast.

With Jean's baby, however, I was fairly matter of fact about the birth. It simply didn't bother me in the same way that I couldn't see what the baby looked like; I didn't care in

126

the same way that I had cared with my own two boys. I didn't make a big fuss or crane my neck to get a good look and see it. I congratulated myself on my control, and registered that it was a boy. But my first thoughts weren't really about the baby at all. They were about Jean.

I looked mainly at her, watched her smiling at the baby. She turned and smiled at me, and I smiled and winked back at her. I would have loved to say something to her, but of course I didn't. We tried not to look at each other in too obvious a manner.

Jean must have seen the way I reacted, and I think she knew at that moment that I would not suddenly surprise her by claiming the baby at the last minute. She must have feared that at least a little all along.

I was feeling pretty dazed at this point, after the delivery and all the gas. They cut the cord and started to clean up the baby. When the cord had been cut, the midwife held the cord in front of my face and said in amazement, 'Will you look at that!' I didn't know what she was talking about, but I just dopily said, 'Oh, yes.'

'There's a perfect knot in it,' she said.

By then my mind had focused a little better and I saw the cord and saw what she was talking about: the cord had a great knot in it.

'Crikey! You're right!' My voice was weak but I was as astounded as the midwife had been. It can't have been more than a few inches away from the baby's own abdomen, which could have been fatal had it tightened and cut off his oxygen supply. I actually felt shocked when I realised that I had only *just* delivered a healthy baby – that I was very, very close to having a stillborn child, just as John would be telling everyone I had. I don't know if Jean was fully aware of the danger we had been in. I was speechless.

But the baby was fine, big and healthy. He weighed 6 pounds 12 ounces. Once they had finished cleaning him, they wrapped him up and put him in my arms. I thought that was unfair: they should have given him to Jean first of all.

I held him and looked at him, but even before I'd had a chance to touch his face or hands, I started feeling what seemed like huge amounts of liquid coming out of me; it felt as if I were going to the loo.

Looking down, I saw that masses of blood was pouring out from between by legs.

'My God!' I said. 'I'm bleeding!' I handed the baby to Jean – which I wanted to do anyway – and turned to the nurse. That bleeding was the only thing I could think about now. The nurses were covered in blood, and I was getting panicky.

'What's going on?' I asked the nurse. 'Why am I haemorrhaging?'

Even the nurse looked astonished. Someone suggested that it had happened because a student midwife had tugged too hard on the cord to deliver the placenta and had torn it away from the uterine wall, which was now bleeding.

Whatever caused it, they got the bleeding under control fast. Someone gave me an injection to stop it and for the first time in my life I didn't mind a bit about the needle going in. I held out my arm for it like a child sticking out her hand for candy. Anything to stop that bleeding. I was having terrible thoughts of stories about women who die in childbirth, and I certainly didn't fancy joining the statistics.

The injection didn't work immediately, but within five minutes the bleeding had slowed down considerably and five minutes after that it was basically stopped. In the meantime, the midwife was poking around inside me to deliver the placenta, and eventually it came out. It was split. They put it on the bed to check that it was all there, and weighed it just to be sure. It was. Finally, when everything was finished, they got round to cleaning me up. I must have been a bit of a mess.

During all this time I had hardly been able to pay any attention at all to Jean and the baby. So much had been happening so quickly. Now I became vaguely aware of Jean talking on the telephone, presumably to Robert.

'It's a little boy,' I heard her say, 'And everything is fine . . . Yes, fine. No, no. It's okay.' I guessed that he was pressing her for details which she couldn't go into at that point. I wondered whether he was asking if the baby looked like him, and if he still wasn't sure that it was his. A little spark of anger came out through my foggy daze.

But in a few moments Jean came back, smiling broadly. The midwife gave her the baby again, and they were both there, Jean holding the little boy in her arms and looking at him with a sweet smile on her face.

'This has been worth it,' I thought to myself. 'That smile makes it all worth it.'

When I was cleaned up, they gave the baby back to me and put me in a wheelchair, and then we were both wheeled along to the ward. Jean pushed the trolley, still smiling sweetly.

On that ride I got my first look at the baby's face. I pushed back the blanket and took a good look at him.

He really was a beautiful baby. He had perfect little features, big wide eyes and a tiny nose and lovely skin. He wasn't wrinkled or red, but had a beautiful colour.

'He's perfect,' I thought to myself.

One interesting thing that I noticed was that he had a fine head of jet-black hair. Both my babies had been bald at birth, and when they grew hair it was a very fine blond.

'That's his father,' I thought. 'Let Robert deny that this is his baby now – it's him all over!'

The fact that he looked so little like my own babies was also good for me. It made me feel more distanced from him. I don't know what I would have felt like if he had been a big, fair baby like my own.

Even so, I did feel a little twinge of envy because he had such a beautiful colour and had such lovely features. He lay there all alert, sucking like mad on his fist with his big eyes wide open, and I couldn't help thinking what a lovely little thing he was.

When we got back to the ward, the baby was put into a cot

beside my bed. Then I was tucked in and Jean pulled up a chair beside me. The nurses brought us tea and left us alone.

*   *   *

Once the baby was in his bed, Jean hardly paid any attention to him. Instead she sat there looking intently at me.

'How are you feeling?' she asked.

I grinned at her, and said that I was fine. Then I reached into my bag and pulled out a card which I had bought specially the week before. The card had taken me hours to find, but I had finally located one, and had carried it around with me for days. It simply said:

JUST WHAT YOU'VE ALWAYS WANTED - A LITTLE BABY

Inside was a picture of a baby with a few lines of verse underneath. No mention of the child's sex, no mention of Mum or Dad. Inside I had written my own little note: 'To Jean and Robert. Congratulations!'

I handed it to her and watched her open it.

Jean looked at the card and read what I had written. She beamed at me. Her eyes seemed to be glistening a little bit - I wasn't quite sure.

'Thank you,' she said. Her voice was choked up. She seemed to like the card. She turned away for a moment.

Then, turning back to me, she asked if I wanted anything, a magazine or some juice or fruit. 'I'll go out to the shops for you if you would like me to.' But I said that I was in for such a short time, it was hardly worth it.

Sitting there with a bare locker next to my bed, I suddenly had a stabbing feeling of self-pity. Normally when you've just had a baby, people come round to see you bringing flowers, chocolate and magazines. I had none of that. I told myself it wasn't necessary, that I had been through all that before, but inside I also felt something of a let-down. Here I

130

had done this amazing thing and there was hardly anyone around to acknowledge it or to cheer me up with nice presents in hospital. That made me feel a little sad. I also wondered if anyone else would wonder why I didn't have all the usual things by my bed, not even flowers. That must have looked a little strange.

But I knew that Jean appreciated me, and her presence was enough to make me feel important – even if I didn't have any flowers by my bed.

By around 10.45 a.m. I was feeling very tired, and I wondered how long Jean was planning to stay. I wanted to take a bath and have a cigarette. Also, I was *dying* to go to the loo but didn't ask because I didn't want the bedpan to be brought to me. So I lay there relaxing with Jean and chatted.

Occasionally she glanced at the cot and I told her that it was okay to pick up the baby if she wanted to. She did this very gingerly, as if she were picked up a vase which she'd been told was worth a fortune. She looked nervous. But she also looked very pleased.

As I watched her, I felt so proud of myself and of what I had done. Jean's eyes sparkled like diamonds as she moved the blanket from the baby's face with her fingers, and she was smiling broadly just as she had done in the labour ward. She was very quiet, very content, and I felt good because I had been the cause of that contentment. I felt as if I were visiting my own sister and her newborn child.

As I watched Jean holding a baby that I had given birth to hours before, it would have been natural for all sorts of bad feelings to arise. Feelings of jealousy, anger, doubt. But there weren't. Instead I was suddenly aware of a closeness between us. It had been so instantaneous that neither of us had even noticed anything unusual. From the moment we were in the labour ward together, it was like a piece of a jigsaw puzzle falling into place. We had become close without even realising it. She had at last got what she most wanted in the world, and I was the one who had enabled her to get it. Very few people are given the opportunity to make someone else that happy.

A little while later Jean went out to phone Robert. When she came back she said that she would go if I wanted her to, but I suggested that she stay for the baby's first feeding. She was happy to stay, and sat back down.

At around 12.30 p.m. I was allowed out of bed to get the baby's bottle. Getting back into bed, I settled myself in. Jean didn't even have to be asked to hand him back for his feeding. She was just there, leaning over to hand him to me automatically. It was all so natural, I might have wondered what I was doing there. But I fed him while Jean watched, and all three of us were perfectly content.

When the feeding was over, Jean said she wanted to go home for a while and that she'd be back for the afternoon visiting hours, which began at 3 p.m. Robert, too, would be coming over in the afternoon.

After she left, the first thing I thought about was going to the loo and having a bath and a cigarette. I was worried that going to the loo would be difficult or painful, as it is sometimes just after you've given birth. Eventually I asked a nurse if I could go, and she said she would bring me a bedpan.

'I'm not going on that!' I told her. 'I want to go *to* the loo.'

After some discussion they said it was all right for me to go, and one of them held my arm. As I walked I felt dizzy all of a sudden, and had to hold on to the door. I was shaking. This was because it had been a shock delivery, and I suppose that in fact I was in shock. I felt cold but was sweating at the same time, and staggering about. But using the toilet was all right, not too painful, and it made me feel much better. I had a wash and went to phone John.

When he answered the phone, his voice sounded sort of nonchalant.

'Well, what's happening? Are you in labour?'

'Not exactly,' I replied. 'I've already delivered it. At
9.45 a.m.'

'What!' There was no more nonchalance in his voice now.
He sounded amazed.

'The baby shot out like a bullet; it didn't want to hang
about. It is a boy.'

When John had recovered a little bit from his shock, he
asked me questions – what the baby looked like, whom it
resembled, whether it was all right. I told him that it had
loads of hair, and that I was sort of peeved about that. I also
told him about the knotted cord and my bleeding, but added
that everything was fine.

'I haven't got any stitches or anything,' I said.

I knew he would be pleased about that. He had hoped the
labour would not be a difficult one.

'And how does Jean feel now?' he asked.

I couldn't say much right there, but I managed to convey
that she was very happy indeed.

'And she took it all right?'

'Cool as a cucumber,' I said. He agreed with me that that
was pretty extraordinary.

'And what about Robert? How has he been?'

'I wouldn't know,' I said. 'He didn't show up – made his
excuses and missed the whole show.' John was very curious
about that, but I couldn't tell him anything more without
arousing suspicion, particularly since the line was very bad
and I almost had to shout to make myself understood. I said
we would have a chance to talk more easily when we were on
our own. But I was glad that John didn't take any of the news
amiss. He seemed pretty cool about it too.

After I hung up the phone I sat there alone in bed, the baby
sleeping in the cot next to me. I felt sleepy myself, but I had
so many things to think about, my mind was too active: it
wouldn't let me sleep. In the end I sat up on the edge of the
bed, pulled the baby's cot over, and looked in.

I was struck once again by the resemblance between him

and Robert. 'He's Robert all over,' I thought. 'He doesn't look anything like me at all.' I was still pleased about that, since it reduced the danger of any real bonding taking place. He was a beautiful baby, and everything had gone fine. But he wasn't my baby; he was Jean's baby.

Jean had hoped it would be a boy, and I was very happy to have given her one. I had been thinking more all along about her happiness than about Robert's, and I'd succeeded in giving her exactly what she wanted. I also took great satisfaction in having predicted it would be a boy: I had never been wrong about the sex of my children before, and now I had kept up my record.

I did feel a certain amount of envy. My own boys had been such big strapping things, and he was much more delicate than they, with finer bones. But this was not a strong feeling, and I did not worry about it very much.

I wondered what Jean was doing now, whether she had gone home and cried or was just feeling all thrilled and excited. And I wondered why Robert hadn't come – was it because he wasn't as brave as he had tried to make out? I thought of when we were in bed together, and he had said he would come along and 'hold my hand' through the whole thing.

'So much for the hand-holding,' I said to myself. 'He couldn't even be bothered to turn up!'

I did feel disappointed about that. Not annoyed, just disappointed. After all, this was one of the most important days in his whole life; perhaps his work could have taken a back seat for once. And it was so important for Jean, how could he go and leave her to do it all on her own? How could he know she would be calm, that she wouldn't get all in a tizzy about it? Apparently such considerations hadn't been important enough to tear him away from his office.

On the other hand, Jean didn't seem to mind his not being there. I had thought she would need his support then more than ever, but obviously I was wrong.

One thing I did while Jean was away was to give the baby a name. I didn't mean to do this, it happened automatically. I didn't know what name Robert and Jean had in mind, but I wanted him to have one so I didn't have to keep calling him 'baby'. I called him Alan, which was a name I happened to like.

It made it easier to talk to him, having that name for him. I knew it was going to be changed of course, but I did think that if I ever had another baby and it was a boy, I would call him Alan.

It's hard to describe what I felt about the baby in those hours. It was love, but a funny kind of love. So-called mother love? A love of his beauty? Or a love of kissing and cuddling and being with him? I still do not know to this day. I certainly didn't feel the same way as I had towards my own boys. Nor did I sense any upswell of longing to keep him for my own. I felt very interested in him, but in a detached sort of way.

The difference undoubtedly lay in the fact that I had produced him with a different father – someone other than John. It's extraordinary what a difference that makes, and how different the babies can be. I spent quite a lot of time thinking about that when I was on my own with Alan.

I also spent a lot of time thinking about my own boys and what I would say to them about their little brother who had been stillborn. I wasn't very worried about doing it, but I wondered what they would say. And I felt sad when I thought of how much fun it would be to actually take a baby home: how happy the family and neighbours would be, how my boys would look at him and play with him, how I'd be able to dress him up and show him off to everybody. Once a mother, always a mother. You think back to when your own were that age and long to be buying all the frilly clothes and other baby things. I'd thought of all this before, naturally, but the feelings became much more intense as I sat there by myself. I didn't feel that I *wanted* to take him home; I just felt

135

sad that I wouldn't be getting any of the fun from him.

I also thought over and over again how lucky I was that it had all gone successfully. After months of worrying about what could go wrong, no major hitches had developed. They could still pop up, naturally, but the worst was over. Thank God for that, I thought to myself.

I was particularly aware of how lucky we had been with the birth. That knotted umbilical cord had really frightened me – we had been so close to losing the baby altogether. My heart thumped even now whenever I thought of it. I had another look at the baby and saw that he really was all right: no blemishes and everything where it should be. I had done a perfect job. But what a close call! Had that cord tightened a bit more we could have lost everything. Thinking about how lucky we had been, I went to sleep.

I think I dozed off, because not much time seemed to have passed. When I woke up, I was surprised to see Jean sitting in the chair by my bed.

'Crikey!' I said. 'Where did you come from? I didn't even hear you.'

'I've only been here ten or fifteen minutes,' she said. 'I didn't want to wake you.'

The strange thing about this was that she wasn't even near the cot, which was at the bottom of the bed; she couldn't see into it from where she was sitting. She had apparently been sitting there all that time looking at me. This was a little disconcerting. Why hadn't she been looking at the baby? What was she was thinking about? Was she afraid or guilty or what? I couldn't bring myself to ask her.

She stayed the rest of the afternoon. Robert was due to arrive at about 4 p.m., and we chatted while waiting for him to show up. Everything seemed to be fine with her: there was no awkwardness or tension in our conversation. I thought again that this natural friendliness was exactly what I had wanted all along. We seemed to have a good rapport, without envy or embarrassment. We talked mostly about childcare and subjects along those lines, and we talked very openly most of the time, even though there were eight or ten other women in the ward. Like us, they all had their curtains drawn, so there was plenty of privacy.

After we had been talking a while, Jean reached into her handbag and pulled out a package.

'Here,' she said as she handed it to me. 'This is something for you.'

I felt embarrassed. I always do when someone gives me a gift. I didn't open it there and then but put it away at the bottom of the bed. I wanted to wait till later to open it. I think she understood; she didn't seem to be hurt, at any rate.

Robert turned up at around 5 p.m., after work. I remained very surprised that he hadn't turned up earlier, and when I finally saw him I felt relieved that he was here at last. He carried a huge bunch of pink carnations, which he gave to me, and also a box of chocolates. He greeted me with a big kiss as he handed over the flowers, then glanced over at Jean.

I suppose that I must have had a smug expression on my face – a sort of 'I told you so' look. I was certainly thinking that, so it must have shown!

Robert himself looked a bit sheepish, though I'm not sure why. Maybe it was for all the things that had gone on before. He had been such a worrier throughout all the preceding months, and he was now looking at me in a way that seemed to acknowledge his foolishness. His look said, 'I know you told me all along that it would work out; please don't remind me.'

Robert didn't look at the baby straight away. In fact, the first five minutes he was there, he and Jean spent most of their time trying to get a vase and some water for the flowers. They both threw themselves into this trivial business with such enthusiasm that it made their nervousness all the more obvious.

Finally, when the carnations were safe in their vase, Robert and Jean both sat down again. Jean was nearest the cot, Robert closer to the head of the bed. After a few moments, she asked him if he was going to look at the baby.

'You ought to, you know. He's beautiful – and he looks just like you.'

Well, Robert tried to act calm about this but you could see that he was excited. He stood up and very carefully walked over to the cot. Looking down at the sleeping baby, he gently poked his finger under the blanket.

Like most fathers, he didn't know what to say. He looked chuffed but also somewhat overawed. 'Well,' he said, and shrugged his shoulders.

'Is that all you've got to say then?' I asked.

He was visibly embarrassed, and shrugged his shoulders again.

'Well, I suppose I'll have to believe it now, won't I?'

We all laughed.

'I suppose you will!' I replied. 'There's no denying that proof in front of you!'

We were all laughing and grinning widely – it was a very happy moment. I was bursting with pride and pleasure that this moment I'd been waiting for had finally arrived. Our conversation was obviously somewhat muted by the fact that there were all those people around, but I knew that we were all thinking the same things. It was lovely to watch Robert's expression, so proud and relaxed and pleased.

'That's how it should be,' I thought. It was the same sort of feeling I had had with Jean just after the birth. At last he was showing happiness, enthusiasm. He was probably wondering even then if I was really going to give them the baby, but his happiness shone through anyway. He was happy that the baby was there.

About ten minutes later the baby woke up. I lifted him out of his cot and handed him to Robert, who held him for a split second and then handed him back. He was nervous because the baby was so small, he said.

I really admired Jean then because she made no attempt

whatsoever to grab the baby, monopolise him in any way or act possessively. I was more impressed by that than I can describe. I was also very grateful for her behaviour in not showing any feelings about me other than warm, friendly ones. I knew that the hormonal changes following birth would make me susceptible to depression, and she did not give me anything to be depressed about. She was really lovely, sweet and good-natured.

Robert and Jean stayed for several hours, chatting and looking at the baby. Neither of them seemed to want to touch him much – maybe because they were still overawed, or maybe they thought it would look strange. Jean was much more natural with him than Robert, but even she didn't really cuddle him properly. She held him in her arms, but not next to her bosom, the way I would have done. I'm sure that was because she didn't want to arouse anyone's suspicions.

By 8 p.m. I was very tired and wanted to be alone and get some rest. I couldn't nod off peacefully with them there, and they seemed to take the hint without my saying anything, because they both stood and up and said they must be going.

As they left, I wondered what they would say to each other once they were outside. What I would have given to be a fly on the wall of their house that night!

I felt a certain admiration for Robert. His doubts and fears seemed to have diminished very fast, and he seemed to be much happier about everything that had gone on between us.

After they left I opened the present that Jean had given me. It was another box of chocolates, some magazines and a lovely pink nightie. I put the nightie on straightaway, then dozed off for a while. When I woke up I had some supper and a cigarette, then went into the day room to talk to the other mums for a while.

The rest of the evening I spent with the baby. I did all the things any woman would do with her newborn baby –

changing, feeding, playing with his fingers and toes and cuddling and talking to him. I enjoyed his company and didn't worry about a single thing.

Finally I went to bed for the night. I lay there in the dark, thankful that the delivery was behind me but a little sad that I wouldn't have all the joys of taking home a newborn baby. My emotions flicked back and forth between a selfish sadness because I would miss out on the fun of a newborn baby, and pride over my delivering a perfect baby and making Robert and Jean so happy. With those thoughts alternating in my mind, I finally fell asleep.

Strangely, a nurse had to wake me when the baby needed feeding in the middle of the night. With my two boys I had been instantly awake the moment they made a sound. This time I was able to distinguish Alan's cry from those of the other babies, but I couldn't wake up on my own. I wondered why this should have been, and supposed that there might be some mental block involved. Anyway, I got up, fed him, changed him, and put him back to bed.

I got afterpains later in the night and sat up to take some Panadol. After that I didn't sleep very well, no matter which way I turned in my efforts to get comfortable.

The only thing I felt really bad about in hospital was that I could not breastfeed the baby. They enjoy that, and I enjoy it. I did it with my two boys, and it comes naturally to me. The first time I gave Alan the bottle I said to him quietly, 'Forgive me for this – it's beyond my control.' I'd never actually discussed the subject with Robert and Jean, but there had been an unspoken agreement about it. I regretted this, but I knew that it made sense: if I had breastfed, the sucking would have produced more milk and then I'd simply have had more trouble getting rid of it. And it would have been cruel to the baby to start out on the breast only to switch over to the bottle.

Also, I had to admit to myself that if I did breastfeed him, that would only increase the bond between us. And I would be denying Jean the pleasure of feeding him herself.

It wasn't only the pleasure of breastfeeding I had to deny Alan. I tended to hold him differently from the way I had held my other boys. With them, I would strip off on top and undo the baby's clothing so that our skin would touch as much as possible. With Alan, I tended to tuck him under the breast, with both of us clothed, so he didn't get the same kind of intimate all-over touching. It was the same sort of handling he would get from a nurse, and that was unfair. I knew that when Jean had had him for a while, she would get the confidence to hold him next to her the way I would have liked to. And the sooner she could start giving the baby what he needed from his mother, the better off Alan would be. With me, he was missing out.

CHAPTER TEN

The Final Days

THE NEXT DAY was fairly routine. I fed and cared for Alan with an expertise that came naturally after having had two babies of my own. All my instincts towards newborns surfaced immediately; it seemed only a matter of hours, not years, since the birth of my last child. The staff mostly left me to it because they knew that this was my third.

'You probably know more about it than I do,' said one student nurse.

I did feel remarkably detached, however – so detached that at times I found myself wondering why I wasn't much more upset about not taking Alan home with me. I had sometimes feared that that would happen, that my feelings might overwhelm me. When they didn't, I was a bit surprised. Perhaps with so much going on at the hospital, all the hygiene and discipline and time-tables, really strong emotions didn't have time to emerge and crystallise. It was all so exhausting that the minute I was on my own all I wanted to do was go to sleep.

Jean arrived at about 4 p.m. I was surprised that she hadn't come at exactly 3 p.m., which was when visiting hours started. She said that Robert was coming at 6 p.m. so she and I spent the next couple of hours talking about childcare.

Jean wanted to know about all sorts of things in more detail – things we had only touched on during the

142

pregnancy, such as formulas for milk and the best types of nappies and so on. It had suddenly become important for her to know about these things in depth. We didn't agree on everything but when we didn't agree she would just say, 'perhaps', and acknowledge my view – while I understood hers.

I thought that the rapport between us was extremely unusual. There was no jealousy or awkwardness. Neither of us rushed over to pick up the baby when he cried; it depended on who happened to get there first. It was so natural. I would have expected both of us to be much more possessive about it.

It was a hospital rule that the baby had to be changed in the nursery, a separate room off the ward where only the parents were allowed. I thought this was unfortunate, since it meant that Jean couldn't see the baby naked or change him herself. This made me sad for her: I know she would have liked to change him. In fact she could have looked at us through a window, but she chose not to. She said she was looking forward to seeing him naked and would wait for that until she could be in the room with him.

So, when I first changed the baby in the nursery, Jean just sat by the bed flicking through a magazine. When I came back I handed him to her straightaway, gave her the bottle and sat with them. I gave her general advice about feeding – how to hold him and the bottle and that sort of thing. I talked very quietly so that people wouldn't think something strange was going on.

While we were sitting there, I called the baby Alan. Jean heard this, and she smiled at me a little quizzically.

'Well, I had to call him something,' I said. 'I couldn't go on calling him baby.'

'Is that the name you would have given him?' asked Jean. She spoke in a soft voice, not angrily or worried at all.

'Yes. That's what I would have called him.'

She didn't respond, and that was the last time we

143

mentioned the subject. I wondered then if they might call him Alan in the end, to please me, or perhaps have it as a middle name. I'm not sure whether I would really have liked that, but I suppose I would have been flattered.

As it turned out, they had their own ideas.

'We were thinking of calling him Jeremy,' Jean said, 'though we haven't decided yet. Not definitely.'

We sat there together very happily, but Robert didn't show up at 6 p.m. By 7 p.m. he still hadn't shown up, and we began to get a little nervous. I was feeling angry and worried, thinking that maybe he wasn't so happy about this after all. When he finally turned up at 7.30 p.m., Jean and I were so on edge that we were both ready to have a go at him.

But as soon as he stepped up to the bed, it became obvious why he had been late: he had been celebrating! His face was flushed, and he looked all excited. I couldn't tell exactly how much he might have had to drink, but he had certainly had a few.

It turned out that Robert had gone round at work telling everyone that he was suddenly a daddy, and after leaving the office he had stood everyone to drinks at a nearby pub. He admitted, somewhat sheepishly, that he had spent over £100 on drinks, but he had such a broad grin on his face as he told us, and he was obviously so happy, that Jean ended up pleased rather than annoyed. She must have been very pleased indeed, not to mind his throwing all that money around.

I felt very pleased too, and very chuffed. Robert was acting normally, like any proud first-time father. He really had drunk a lot, and he was acting like it – beaming away, talking loudly, swaggering about. He was making it clear that he was the father of the baby in the cot.

'Isn't he handsome,' Robert would say. 'Looks just like his dad, don't you think? Spitting image!'

Which was all very well, except that Robert was supposed to be my brother, not my husband. What on earth must the people nearby have been thinking?

Jean and I did our best to calm him down without drawing even more attention to the happy family scene, but it really was funny. There was Robert, stinking of booze, coochy-cooing, and announcing to the whole ward that he was the father of a baby who everyone else thought was his nephew. When he finally stopped dribbling over the cot, he came over and sat down on the bed and put his arms around me. I told him to shut up but he wasn't having any of it! Even when the bell went off announcing that visitors should leave, he wouldn't budge. Half-an-hour later he was still there babbling away at the top of his voice.

I couldn't be angry about this, even though I did worry that the woman in the bed next to me would hear what Robert was saying. Seeing Robert unable to control his happiness made the embarrassment worthwhile. Eventually, at around 8.45 p.m., the nurse came round and suggested that they had stayed a long time. Robert didn't want to go, but eventually Jean did manage to drag him away. They both gave me a kiss, and said they'd be round the next morning to collect me. No one asked any questions about Robert, so my fears proved groundless.

After they left, I felt great. That evening had been a happy one for all of us, with nothing but good feelings between Robert and Jean and me. As I fell asleep, I wondered whether the good feelings would continue.

*   *   *

The next morning I got up and had a bath and some breakfast. I don't like hospitals so I was excited to be leaving, but I kept wondering what was going to happen next, when we went to Robert's and Jean's house. What would the relationship between us be like then? What was I going to do with myself all day? How was I going to keep out of the way? I even worried about what I would be eating, and what would happen if Jean wasn't a good cook or cooked things that I didn't like. And would she get upset when I had to take charge of the baby because the midwives were coming? These were all thoughts I had had during the pregnancy and they were still unresolved. It was a Saturday. I would have to stay with Robert and Jean until at least the next Saturday or Sunday, depending on the midwives' visits. A week was a long time.

Jean had brought in baby clothes the day before, and I fed and changed Alan before she and Robert were due to arrive. I had great fun doing that, dressing him up and making him look nice. Then I put him in his cot and he quickly fell asleep.

Once Alan was taken care of I packed my own things, then sat down and waited. Robert and Jean didn't turn up for some time – they got caught in traffic – which meant that I had to wait alone. I didn't like that, sitting there and twiddling my thumbs, but I waited as patiently as I could. Every so often I would look in the cot and check to make sure that Alan was all right. He slept soundly the whole time.

After Robert and Jean arrived, we got organised for the drive to their house. I wondered whether I should give Alan to Jean so she could carry him out of the hospital herself. In the end I decided that I should do it myself. It was only a little thing, but there was no point in taking chances at this stage.

I went to check with the staff to make sure it was all right for me to leave. It was fine. They were very business-like with me because I was an experienced mother: they didn't even insist that I have an escort to the door, as I had thought they might. We just said goodbye and that was that. No fuss. I couldn't help thinking that they would have made more of a fuss if they had known where the new arrival was headed once we waltzed out the door!

I felt a little strange being in street clothes. I was still a bit weak after the birth, and walked slowly down the corridor and through the hospital foyer. When we got to the car,

146

Robert opened the door of the back seat for me and I got in with the baby. Jean got in next to me while Robert drove.

By this time the hormonal depression had started setting in. You don't feel depressed from this in the usual sense, like when you're just feeling low about something. It's a much more vague, unfocused feeling; you cry for no apparent reason. You can't help it. It just happens.

This time it happened to me as soon as I got into the car. The relief of getting out of hospital, the strangeness of the situation, my uncertainty about what was going to happen next, they all must have come crashing down on me like an avalanche. The hormones let go, and I started to cry.

Jean didn't say anything, she just sat there quietly. And she didn't try to take Alan from me, as I had supposed she would. I clutched him in my arms as the tears started flowing, and Robert drove on with his eyes fixed firmly on the road. After a while Jean put her arm gently around me and tried to comfort me. She was really wonderful then – her only thought was to console me. I don't know if she felt guilty about the situation, if she thought I was crying because it was coming to the crunch, but I suppose she did realise that I wouldn't be in this distress if it weren't for her, and she must have felt some responsibility for that.

Finally I cried myself out. It took quite a few minutes, but after that I regained my composure and felt all right. By the time we got to their house it was all over.

I hadn't been to their new house, and I was looking forward to seeing it. We entered through the basement, which led directly into a big kitchen with an adjoining dining area. I carried Alan while Robert and Jean took my bags. I sat down with the baby, and Jean went straight to the kettle to make a cup of tea. We drank it together, me still holding the baby on my lap.

Jean seemed to come into her own once we were at the house: she felt confident and in control of things. The place was spotless and very tidy.

147

'I suppose I'd better get some bottles ready or something,' she said. 'They've got to be sterilised.'

It was still two hours before Alan's next feeding time, so I told her there was no rush.

'But you might as well get them ready,' I added. 'No harm in that. Would you like me to show you how to do it?'

'Yes, please,' she replied. She was eager to learn, which I thought was great. They got their new carrycot and we put the baby in it and left him there while I showed Jean how to sterilise the bottles. Then we sat back down and chatted, mainly about the new house. They were still doing it up, and we talked about all the different things they were planning. I told them how much I liked what they had decided on.

'It will be a nice house for a child to grow up in,' I said. They liked that.

'I'll show you around in a minute,' said Robert. After I'd shown Jean how to make the feeds up and how to make them up in advance for night feeding, we went through the house from top to bottom.

The room where I was to stay was right at the top. It was decorated very nicely and had a little colour television for me to watch, just as Jean had promised. I thought I would be able to feel pretty comfortable there, and I said this to Robert.

'I'd like to see the baby's room next,' I added. 'I'll need to know all about it and the baby's things when the midwives come here.'

'Of course,' said Robert. The baby's room was next door to mine, and was also done up very nicely with baby things and a pale blue wallpaper. Jean had put a bed in there because she intended to sleep with the baby for the first few weeks, until she got used to him, so that Robert wouldn't be woken up when she gave him his night feeds.

One thing did make me very happy and very at ease: from the minute the baby was born, I had felt a change for the better in my relationship with Robert and Jean. We had become less suspicious and much more friendly and

148

trusting. That change had continued, and I still felt it now as Robert took me round the house. We communicated with each other in a different way.

That evening we were all tired out from the excitement and newness of it all. I went to bed at around 9.30 p.m. and watched television for a while, then fell asleep at around 10.15 p.m.

Before going to bed I had told Jean that she should wake me if she needed any help with the baby during the night. She did come in, at about 2 a.m., but I think that was more for moral support than for any specific practical guidance. She was coping very well with the baby, as I could see. And after that she did everything herself, not waking me at all.

I only woke up myself once, on the second night. Suddenly I found myself awake, and didn't know why for a split second, until I heard the baby crying. The biological connection between us had woken me automatically.

I listened to him for a while, then the crying stopped. Jean didn't call me or come in, so I knew he was being fed and looked after. I felt surprisingly little urge to go and see if he was all right – I knew that his well-being was guaranteed by Jean's care – and went back to sleep. After that I never woke up again when he cried in the night. Jean was his mother now, and I did not want to intrude on her privacy with him when they were alone together. One result of this was that I slept well every night and therefore recovered from the birth much more quickly than I would have done ordinarily. I was never tired my whole stay there. Jean took over the exhaustion when she took over Alan.

Over the next few days, life at the house settled down into an easy, relaxing routine. This surprised me: I had expected it to be much more difficult. Since I had come out of hospital at a weekend, Robert was around for the first two days, but after that he was away during the day. He told me before he left for work on the Monday that he was glad I would be there to keep Jean company in those first important days.

For me, once he was gone for the day, it was very much like spending the day at a friend's house. Jean and I didn't bother to get dressed, got up when we pleased and went around all day in our dressing-gowns. Sometimes she got up to make breakfast, sometimes I did. We were both very relaxed about everything. Most of the day we spent in the kitchen. I'd smoke a cigarette and we would chat away like old pals about this and that, especially the baby and his needs. When we went upstairs we would take the carrycot with us or keep the intercom on if we left the baby in the kitchen. If he cried while one of us was doing something, the other would go to see what he needed. There was no discussion, we just did it that way.

We usually saw to feeding and changing him together. This happened naturally, with no pushing or shoving to get there first. Whoever felt like it at the time would feed him. Generally I made sure that Jean fed him herself, though she was equally willing and happy to have me do it. Neither of us felt guilty about doing it ourselves or jealous when the other did it. Our 'shared care' system seemed to be working perfectly. It certainly helped make me feel like less of an outsider – more like, say, a paternal aunt helping a new mother to settle down with her charge.

Alan had very quickly become Jeremy. The afternoon of our first day back from hospital, they told me they had definitely decided on the name. For the time being, however, I continued to call him Alan. This made him seem like a different baby, easing the changeover quite a lot. The name change, plus the fact that he was so dark and unlike my own blond boys, made it almost easy to separate myself from him. But I was proud of him all the same, because he really was a very nice baby. He was very alert and intelligent, with good muscle coordination and tone.

*   *   *

On the morning of my second day there, the midwife came

150

round. We were nervous about her coming, and spent some time fabricating a story to explain why I was staying with Robert and Jean. She was a jolly, middle-aged woman with a ruddy complexion, not threatening-looking at all.

As it turned out, she didn't give us a chance to tell our story. She clearly assumed without a second thought that I was Robert's wife, and she could not care less about our domestic arrangements. She only wanted to make sure that mother and baby were doing well. Since she didn't ask questions, it soon became obvious that we should let her go on thinking whatever she wanted to. Trying to 'set her straight' with lengthy explanations would only complicate matters.

Jean left the room as the midwife prepared to examine me, but Robert stayed. He assumed that if the midwife thought he was the father of the baby, it would be normal for him to listen to what she said and take an interest in what went on. I cursed him for that. I was terrified that I would be given a physical examination and that it would look odd if he turned his back – but I didn't want him watching, either. I was still bleeding, and I knew I would be terribly embarrassed. Luckily for me, she didn't want to examine me down below that day. She took my temperature and felt my uterus through the nightie I was wearing. I felt very relieved about that.

After that, a midwife came every day. If it wasn't the original one it was another. Neither of them asked many questions, simply did what was necessary to make sure the baby and I were all right. The younger one did ask once where my other children were, and I lied and told her they were staying with their grandmother so that I could establish a routine with the new baby without their feeling neglected. That seemed to satisfy her, and she didn't ask anything more about them. Nor did I volunteer much other information, apart from chatting a little about 'my' new house, and doing it up, little things like that.

151

It amazed me that this part of the plan passed so easily, with hardly a hitch. Nothing about the set-up seemed to arouse the slightest suspicion in the midwives. They accepted everything without blinking an eye. Jean and I had both been more worried about this phase than about anything else, and not a single problem arose. We counted ourselves very lucky indeed.

Jean and I did a little cooking together. Normally their tastes in food were fancy, too foreign for my taste. But they made an effort to have things that I liked, so mainly we ate roasts, beef or chicken with plain vegetables. And I showed her how to make a few of the simple English dishes I like, such as shepherd's pie and Lancashire hot pot. My fears about eating well were certainly proved unnecessary.

When we ate together in the evenings, most of the talk was about the baby. He was being a bit difficult, and Jean had made a habit of demand-feeding him with the bottle. I agreed with that in principle, since feeding them a full bottle when they are hungry means they'll have a good sleep and wake up when they're hungry again. But the baby was taking only a little bit of food at each feeding, then waking up a half-hour later hungry for another feed. I believe in demand-feeding but not in every-half-hour feeding.

'You'd better watch out for that,' I told Jean. 'If it keeps up you'll be forever feeding him and messing with him and you'll never get any time to yourself.' A routine was important, I said. 'Keep trying and you'll get him on a regular eating schedule.'

Jean tried, but she couldn't do it.

'When I put the bottle to his lips he won't take it. It doesn't work.'

When I saw her try, I knew what the problem was: she gave up immediately he pursed his lips to reject the bottle, and didn't persevere at all. She made no effort to coax him into taking it. This went on for five days or so, and she was starting to get tired – even though I was doing half of it. I

152

didn't push the matter. He was her baby, not mine; it wasn't for me to interfere in the way she wanted to do things. All I could do was provide general advice and leave it at that.

But by the fifth day the baby was still feeding very irregularly, and Jean was getting worried. So I broke my own rule and asked if she would like me to force him into a routine.

'How can you do that?' she asked.

'Well, it's really very simple. You starve him. Give him a bottle at a certain time – one in the morning is good – and then simply don't give him any more until a minimum of three hours has passed.'

'But isn't that cruel?'

'It's a bit cruel, but in the end it's better than letting things go on as they have done. It will force him into a routine and then your life will be a lot easier.'

Jean agreed reluctantly, making it clear that she wanted me to be the one doing the dirty work. I fed him, then just sat back to wait three hours. After a while the baby started crying and Jean got very upset. I could see her counting the minutes until the feed would be due. We took turns cuddling him, winding him, changing his nappy, and keeping him occupied while he was awake. When he was alseep we would put him down, then start the whole thing over again when he woke up. I gave him a little bit of boiled water or caraway seed water until he settled down again. Eventually it was time for another bottle, and he would drink hungrily but only take half the bottle, then start nodding off immediately. I'd tickle his feet and hands and wind him, trying to keep him awake.

While I was trying to introduce this routine into the baby's feeding, we discovered that he didn't like having his nappy changed. He got very upset when the air came in contact with his backside, yelling lustily every time we started to change him and keeping it up until we had a new nappy on. Then one of us would cuddle him and he calmed down. Our

153

solution was to change him quickly whenever he nodded off during the midst of a feed, but even then he would wake up and start bawling. So we would feed, then wind, then feed again, and just when he wouldn't be coaxed any more we would change him. We also really annoyed him by washing his backside and fiddling with him until he really began yelling. Then it was downstairs to the kitchen again, by which time he'd take the rest of the bottle.

After two days of that he started, at long last, to get into the routine. Doing all of this was very hard for Jean: she didn't like forcing the baby to do anything he didn't want to do. But she agreed that I had the experience, and that it was probably a good thing after all. We discussed this sort of thing endlessly at mealtimes.

During that first week, Jean suffered from the exhaustion that all new mothers have. She stayed up all day as well as all night to look after the baby, and she got extremely tired. She was living on nervous energy, and never put on any make-up because she was so tired. I told her she should take naps during the day and let me look after the baby. At first she didn't want to do this, but she changed her mind the next day and had a rest. She went upstairs to have a bath and got into bed at about 4 p.m. I saw to the baby's needs and then sat reading a book in the living-room, going upstairs to see Alan when I heard him crying. I fed him and changed him and sang to him a little, and he finally fell asleep again. Meanwhile Jean managed to fall asleep at around 5 p.m.

*   *   *

I rang John every night. It was great talking to him, but also very frustrating because I couldn't talk to him openly about a lot of what was going on. For example, John always asked about Robert and Jean – especially Jean, how she was enjoying the baby and everything. I couldn't say anything personal about them for fear that one of them might

154

overhear. I did say that I was getting along much better with Robert, particularly since he wasn't teasing me as I had worried he might. And I did say that Jean was most definitely enjoying the baby.

John mentioned that a number of bills had come in, and asked if Robert was going to be giving me some money straightaway.

'We could use it to pay those bills,' he said.

'I know,' I replied. 'And Robert will be giving me some money. Don't worry about it.'

'I'm not worried, just wondering.'

As much as I missed John, talking to the boys was even more difficult. I spoke to them the first time I rang, and found that I couldn't keep myself from getting all weepy. The eldest had only said they missed me, and asked when I was coming home. He didn't even mention the baby. But his question really got to me, and I choked up all of a sudden. He heard me, and asked me what the matter was.

'It's nothing, darling, I just miss you too.'

After that I decided not to talk to them until I actually got home. It was too hard for me, and I didn't think they were finding it very easy either. So I only talked to John after that.

* * *

Having lived in their house such a short time, Robert and Jean did not know any of their neighbours very well. Jean had partly planned it this way, wanting to keep them at a distance so they wouldn't ask any questions before the baby arrived. Now it seemed that she would probably be more friendly because she said she had never made any friends in their old neighbourhood, and she hated that. Not going to work made her just a housewife like any other, except that she was childless. That made her different, an outsider. She had too much time to dwell on her sadness, and didn't like to associate with the neighbours because they all had kids of their own. In her new house, she decided, she would be friendlier with everyone. And having the baby would make it easier for her to do that, as well as giving her a reason to *want* to be friendly.

Since Robert's and Jean's closest friends and relatives knew about the baby, the house was filled with the flowers they had sent. This was very nice for me. I had some lovely things in my room.

Their openness with friends and family did produce a few little complications. Robert's father, who is retired, had done a lot of the decorating in the baby's room: he had volunteered for the job and liked the feeling of being involved. But now that the baby was here, he wanted to come over and meet me. Robert had invited him, but he was opposed to the idea: he thought it would be easier for his parents to accept the baby as Jean's if they didn't meet the natural mother, and always pictured Jean as the 'real' mother. Personally, I wasn't bothered either way, but in the end they didn't come.

Other people did come, among them Jean's best friend. They all brought flowers and little presents of clothes and things for the baby.

Jean had her birthday while I was staying there, and I sneaked out to buy her a present. I always try to buy presents that are right for the recipient, just what they would like, and I went round to a lot of places before I found something for Jean. One little shop had a vanity case which I thought she might like. I bought that, but it didn't seem enough of a present for her. Finally, in a clothes shop, I found what I wanted. Jean had mentioned that she didn't have a dressing-gown that she really liked, and I saw one that I thought would be perfect for her – a full-length gown that was thin and floaty enough to wear in a centrally heated house like theirs. I folded it up and put it inside the vanity case.

Jean seemed to love it. She's not like me with presents: she didn't say thanks and then put it away, but changed into it straightaway and wore it until she got dressed later in the morning. The next day she wore it again.

I had wanted to get her a birthday cake as well, but there wasn't a bakery nearby that had any. Robert and Jean didn't do much to celebrate the occasion, so the lack of a cake didn't seem to make much difference to them. We had supper together in the evening as usual, nothing special.

In the evening of my fifth day there, over dinner, Robert brought up the subject of registering the baby with the doctor in the area. They had already registered themselves, and the baby had to be registered too. We discussed the pros and cons of doing it now or waiting until I was gone. The doctor had Jean's records, and he obviously knew that she was incapable of having a baby; and, anyway, she hadn't been pregnant when she registered weeks before. Obviously he would want to know where the baby had come from. Robert was worried that if he told the story that I'd told my GP, he might not be believed. They might think that Robert and Jean had snatched the baby or something, and then the welfare workers would be round to investigate. Robert thought it might be best to register now.

'If we tell the doctor now,' he said, 'we can tell him that the natural mother is here, and he can confirm our story if he wants to.' He thought we could say that the mother was someone other than Jean, and that they were adopting with the natural mother's consent.

From the way he said this, I could tell he wasn't trying to push the matter too hard against my wishes and, because of that, I agreed that that would be all right with me. I actually thought it was a good idea for other reasons. First, if the doctor did want to confirm the story, I would rather it happened now, while I was staying with them, rather than letting the doctor know my address. Second, Robert was worried about it, and I could see that it would give him peace of mind to register the baby as soon as possible. So I agreed, and he made an appointment for the next day.

He came back from the doctor with a great big smile on his

face. There had been no problems at all, he said. He had told the same story I'd told, and the doctor had said it was all fine. The doctor had taken all the details of the birth, and said that there was no reason why anyone else had to have them. So that was another problem out of the way, and I was very pleased that this too had gone so easily. I was a little worried about the health visitor, but luckily she was attached to that same doctor's surgery, and he was going to brief her about the situation. So the secret would be confined to the two of them.

The next step was formal registration of the baby, which had to take place within forty-two days of the birth. Robert and I went along to the registry office together. I wanted us to go together because I wanted Robert to see that I had registered the baby in the right way. I also thought it would be best for them to have a birth certificate in their name. So we registered the baby, under Robert's surname, giving Robert as the father and me as the natural mother. The only slightly illegal thing I did was to give their address as my own so that I couldn't be traced. This didn't matter greatly because I had been living there for several days and would be for several days more.

I did feel a little funny registering the baby under the name of Jeremy, a name that I hadn't chosen myself. If I'd wanted to I could have registered him as Alan, and then let Robert and Jean change the name when the adoption went through. But I never seriously considered doing this.

Robert seemed especially bouncy and cheerful after we had been to the registry office. I suppose that it just hit home to him that I really was doing everything I said I would do. Afterwards he went off to work and I went back to their house to show the birth certificate to Jean.

'Look,' I said to her. 'He's all legal now! He's your baby!' Robert and Jean were so pleased and proud about that birth certificate. I'd never seen anyone look so pleased about a piece of paper before.

158

The eight days I spent at Robert's and Jean's were very beneficial for me, I think. Jean and I got on so well together the whole time that I did not feel left out or threatened in any way. Had the baby disappeared from my life immediately, leaving me completely ignorant of how he was being cared for or the environment in which he was being brought up, I would probably have felt the loss much more keenly. As I participated so fully in those first days, I was able to see Alan as Jeremy, *their* child, and the giving of that child was more of a joy than a wrenching loss.

But, as the days passed, I began to worry about leaving. I was enjoying myself immensely looking after this baby, and I was enjoying Jean's company too. I liked her very much as a person, and I was so pleased that everything had gone so well that I was worried about how I would feel when I finally went home and the baby was no longer there with me. Would I regret it and feel let down? I worried about this more and more.

I also began to realise that I was unlikely to see the baby for a long time. Although in the early days we had all said we would go on being friends, Robert and Jean had not mentioned this again and I got a strong sense that they did not want to. It was up to them; I wasn't going to say anything about it myself.

When the midwife came on the Thursday, I asked her how many more visits she was planning to make. They can come for up to twenty-eight days, though ten (including the days in hospital) is more normal. I said that I was wondering because we had relatives coming to stay, but didn't want them until she was finished with her visits.

To my complete surprise, she said that this was her last. I had thought she would be calling one more time at the very least, but understood what had happened when I caught a glimpse of her form. She had written that I'd come 'home' on day 3, and when the midwife came the next day, she had mistakenly written that that was day 5 instead of day 4.

In any case, I was to get only five days instead of six. That meant that I could leave as early as Friday morning, but we decided that it could be unwise for me to leave them. When the midwives checked their records they might see their mistake and want to see me on Friday after all. If they came back then and I wasn't there, the situation might look strange to them. So we decided that I should stay until Friday evening at least. Robert said that he would come back from the office early.

* * *

Friday morning I got up at around 8.30 a.m. and went out to buy the baby a gift. I searched for a while before finding a musical ball with a picture of Snow White and the Seven Dwarves. I had noticed that Robert and Jean hadn't bought one of these. Babies like them, in my experience. When I returned to the house, I wrapped up the ball in blue tissue paper.

Then I sat down and wrote the baby a three-page letter. I had thought about doing this, and decided I wanted something for the baby to remember me by. His parents would be telling him about me, about his special conception and the woman who had given birth to him, and I wanted him to have something from me – something he could read for himself when he learnt the truth about his origins.

I told him that he was not an abandoned baby. He was a carefully planned baby, and although I was his biological mother, his real mother was Jean, who had brought him up and cared for him over the years. 'Do not pine for me,' I wrote, 'someone you have never met, but love and respect your parents.' I told him that he should respect his parents all the more now that he knew how much they had had to fight for him. He was welcome to contact me if he wanted to,

160

if he really could not contain his curiosity, but he should remember above all who his real mother was – in the loving and not just the biological sense.

'I love you deeply, in a strange way, but I feel no regret about what has happened. The whole relationship between your parents and me was warm and special. You are a very special boy.' I did not know how to sign it, so in the end I didn't sign it at all.

I put the letter in an envelope and sealed it. As I did so, I wondered when it would be opened, and what the young stranger reading it would be like. I wanted Robert and Jean to give him the letter when he was old enough to understand. I only hope that my own kids will understand why I did it, if and when I have to tell them.

By noon, when the midwife had still not come, I assumed that she was not going to come. I packed my suitcase and cleared up my room, determined to leave it as I'd found it. Jean had been pottering about for a while doing housework, and at around 12.30 p.m. we fed the baby and had some lunch. I was feeling quiet and subdued, and so was Jean. Neither of us said very much.

Robert arrived at 4 p.m. We all had a cup of tea together and agreed that I could now go home if I wanted to.

'When would you like to go?' Jean asked.

'I don't mind,' I said. 'I could go anytime, I suppose.'

'Well, there's no hurry,' Jean replied. 'Not for us. Why don't you stay for a couple of hours, at least until the next feed's done, anyway?' I was happy she made that offer, and said I would stay for a while. Alan was due for a feed shortly. I phoned John and told him I would be back at around 6 or 7 p.m. He asked if he should come and collect me, but I said that I would rather get a cab.

Jean and I went in together to give Alan his feed. I could tell straight off that he needed a change, too, so I took off his nappy and cleaned him up.

Usually when I was with Jean I didn't really give Alan a

161

good kiss or a proper cuddle. I generally did when he and I were alone. I don't think she would have liked my doing this very much – she's very germ-orientated, and she never really approved of my smoking. But this time I thought to myself, 'Well, this is the last chance I'll get.' So while he was naked I kissed him all over and nuzzled him and sniffed his lovely baby smell and cooed over him.

Jean smiled while all this was going on. She didn't seem to mind at all. When I had finished and put him down, she had the bottle ready.

'Here you are,' she said as she handed it to me.

I started to take it, then changed my mind.

'No, you give him this feed. Here.' I handed Alan over to her, then sat down on the edge of the bed.

Jean took Alan and looked at me. I looked at her, and at Alan, and I started to cry.

I couldn't stop myself: all that emotion was too much for me. I had known this would happen, but somehow until the moment arrived I couldn't imagine what it would be like. I'm a tough person in some ways, but underneath I'm very soft. This had got right to the soft bits. I cried uncontrollably for several minutes.

'What do I do now?' I asked myself in despair. I felt no regret for what I was doing, but that isn't the same thing as feeling no sense of sadness at all. I would miss Alan – miss looking after him. And judging by Robert's and Jean's silence on the subject, this was probably the last time I would ever see him, at least until he was grown-up, and the helpless little baby I had just cuddled was worlds away. I realised as I sat there crying that I didn't have a picture of him. I wondered if they would give me one.

Jean acted all quiet when I began crying, then carried on feeding the baby and pretending she hadn't noticed. She asked me midway through if I wanted to finish the feed, but I said no.

'I think it's best if I go,' I said. 'I'll wait downstairs till you're done.' This was much better than making Jean feel rotten when she didn't deserve to feel that way. I got my bags from my room and went down the stairs, still crying. As much as I didn't want to, I couldn't help myself. There was too much sadness in me to keep bottled up. I had no choice whatsoever.

Robert was in the kitchen, and he could obviously see that I was crying. He didn't say anything, just asked if I wanted more tea. I said I'd make myself one.

After a few minutes' silence he finally spoke again.

'Are you all right, Kirtsy?' His voice was kind and gentle.

'Yes,' I said. I took out a cigarette and lit it. My own voice was all croaky. 'I'm fine. I promised myself I wouldn't cry while I was here, but now that I am, you'll just have to accept it.' I added, after a pause, 'Sorry.'

'You don't need to apologise,' he said. 'I understand.' I had never heard such softness in his voice before.

We sat there for ten minutes. Mostly we were silent except for my sobbing, which had subsided now and wasn't so regular. Finally I spoke up again.

'I'll be going soon. I'd better call a cab.'

Robert knew I was going, but this seemed to catch him off his guard. He took a deep breath, as if he were beginning a big long important speech.

'You know how grateful we are to you for what you've done,' he said. 'But I don't think you really appreciate how far that gratitude goes.' I stubbed out my cigarette and stared into my tea so I wouldn't have to look at him. I didn't know what to say.

'The giving of the baby meant more to us than just having a baby. What you've given to Jean is a life.'

I was blushing furiously. I lit another cigarette and kept staring down at my knees.

'It's a life for both of us, really,' he went on. 'Without you... without the baby... I don't know what future for Jean and me there would have been. She was so depressed

163

about not having a child, I don't think we could have carried on like that much longer . . .' His voice sort of trailed off at the end.

I didn't know what to say to any of this. I thought that if I spoke I'd just start my crying. Again it was Robert who broke the silence.

'Thank you. Thank you for everything.'

Finally I looked at him and saw that he was grinning sheepishly. I managed a smile myself, through my tears.

'At least you believe me now,' I said. 'I've kept my promise.' He smiled at that.

'Oh, I have something for you,' he said after a moment. And he handed me a little package which I assumed had my next payment in it. 'Quick, put it in your handbag.' He seemed to want it out of the way as soon as possible.

When I had put it away, he carried on thanking me. I was acutely embarrassed still, but at least my tears had dried up. I even managed to say a few words myself about how pleased and proud and happy I was for them. I said I hoped they would have a wonderful life together and that they felt that everything they had been through had been worth it.

'And I hope', I concluded, 'that you're pleased with what you've got.'

Robert grinned broadly.

'Pleased? We're ecstatic. Jeremy is a perfect baby. And I know that Jean thinks so too. We couldn't have asked for anything more. Nothing at all.'

We heard Jean coming down the stairs then, and Robert and I smiled at each other. Jean was by herself – she had left the baby upstairs, for which I was grateful. I didn't want to start crying again.

Jean sat down and we had a chat. They promised that they would send me a photograph of the baby as soon as they had one. Both of them were looking very serious out of consideration for my feelings, but I broke the ice by making a little joke about my crying.

'I intentionally didn't put on mascara this morning, you know. I knew I would be having a good cry, and I didn't want a smudged face.' We had a laugh about that.

I could have gone upstairs to say goodbye to the baby, but I decided not to. I had done that earlier in the day, and didn't want to make myself worse again by stirring up the sad feelings. So I said again to them both, 'I hope you'll be very happy,' and Jean gave me a little parcel of presents for my children. Then, without saying another word, I went over to phone a cab.

We assumed that the cab would take ages, as they always do, but this one arrived in ten minutes. All in a rush, I gave them the present for Alan and my letter, and thanked them again for everything.

'Let me take your bags,' Robert offered.

'No, that's all right. I'll manage.' We gave each other kisses and they walked me to the door. I walked out alone to the cab, Robert and Jean standing on the doorstep.

Halfway down the path I turned to them one last time.

'See you again,' I called.

The cabbie took my big bag in the front seat, and I trundled into the back. As I slammed the door behind me, I noticed that a light rain was falling. Robert and Jean were still on the doorstep, huddled together against the chill.

The cab had been driving only a couple of moments before I started crying again. This time I really didn't know why – the strangeness and excitement of it all, I suppose. Everything was happening so fast. I wondered if I would see Alan again. I had hoped that Jean and I would continue our friendship, but thought that this must be an unrealistic hope. She hadn't said anything about our seeing each other again. It would be too difficult, in the circumstances. This made me feel sad, because of the closeness I thought we had developed.

'At least they're good people,' I thought. 'The baby will be in good hands with them.' I knew that Jean, after her years of

165

longing for a child, would be a good mother when it came down to it.

But that was behind me now. I was going home. I was going to see my own boys, and I wanted to calm myself down before I got there.

*   *   *

John was standing on our doorstep when the cab pulled up. He came down and paid the driver, then carried my bags up to the house. When we got there, he gave me a great big hug. I immediately burst into tears. My boys were running down the stairs to me and giving me their own hugs. The four of us stood there together on the doorstep. I couldn't stop crying.

'Why are you crying?' the older boy asked me.

'It's because I've missed you so much,' I answered. 'Because I've missed you and I'm so glad to see you. Are you glad to see me too?'

'Yes, yes!' both boys yelled in unison. I was surprised to see that the older boy's eyes were dry: he normally starts crying at the first glimmer of a tear in my eyes. I think he probably realised I was happy to see him, and therefore didn't need to cry.

We went inside, and I calmed myself down. John went to put the kettle on, and the question I had been expecting came out. It was the younger one who said it.

'Where's the baby?'

John had come back from the kitchen, and we looked at each other.

'You didn't say anything?' I asked him.

'No.' I had to do it all myself.

Taking both the boys in my arms, I knelt down and told them that I wasn't bringing the baby home.

'Why?' asked the younger one.

'Because the baby has gone to Heaven.'

They stood there, silent. Then the older boy spoke again.

166

'Do you mean it's dead?'

'Well... yes,' I said. I hadn't expected to have to use that word.

'Why is it dead?'

Because it was very, very sick.' I didn't want to put too much emphasis on the sickness because the older boy has asthma and I didn't want him to think that he might die.

'It's not like you're sick,' I quickly added. The baby was *very* sick, too sick to live here with us. So he's gone to live with God and God will look after him.'

'How did he get up there?'

'God came down and got him' I replied.

'Did you see Him?' asked the older one.

'No, you can't see God. He comes and gets people when you're not looking.'

'Is he magic?'

'Well, yes,' I replied. 'He's invisible, so you can't see him. He pops down from Heaven on his ladder but no one can see him, but we know he's there, and he's taken the baby back up with him.' I gave the boys another hug.

'But don't worry,' I said. 'We'll try to grow another one, okay?'

'Okay, mummy.' The older boy spoke for both of them, and they cuddled a little closer.

John was very pleased to have me back. He proudly showed me some work he had been doing on the house, and pointed out how clean he had kept the place in my absence. Which indeed he had: it was spotless, and all the ironing and washing was beautifully done.

John said he had told as many people as he could the sad news, and we had had several kind letters of condolence from the neighbours, which touched me. I rang John's parents that evening and told them it was all over, and they too were very kind and concerned. I felt bad lying to all these people – that was undoubtedly the worst aspect of the whole thing. But by this time I was used to the idea that I had to. There

167

simply wouldn't be any point in telling them the truth.

In the hall was a huge bouquet of flowers which had been sent by my old boss and colleagues. They had known when the baby was due and John had not had the heart to tell them the lies he told everyone else. A gaily coloured card lay beside the vase congratulating me on the birth of my new baby. 'Hope you'll come and visit us all soon,' it said. I winced as I read that. There was no point in telling them the truth that wasn't a truth, either – that the baby was stillborn. A feeling of exhaustion swept over me. I hugged my two little boys to me tight as I fought back more tears.

*   *   *

That night I went to bed exhausted, good and ready for a long sleep. I felt shattered and drained. But I also felt a kind of victorious feeling. I had followed through a plan I had hatched over a year before, and now two people were happier than they had ever been – because of me. A little feeling of excitement came over me, even in my exhaustion. I had been on a great adventure, something that few other women would experience. It had been hard at times, but finally it had been worth it. And I had ended up where any adventurer is supposed to finish his wanderings: at home, and in my own bed. I was very happy to be there.

CHAPTER ELEVEN

Six Months Later:
Events and Afterthoughts

AN ENVELOPE IS lying on the hall table. In it is a cheque for £5,000 made out to Robert and Jean. I am giving back all the money I have received from them.

I've been advised to do so by a lawyer who is organising my side of the adoption. After I explained the situation to him, he told me I was treading on dangerous ground. Even if I claimed that the money was compensation for loss of earnings, he said, a court might decide that in fact it was payment for a private adoption. That's illegal.

The fine I could have received for accepting the money was only about £400, but a court case might jeopardise Robert's and Jean's adoption of Alan. I could never do anything that might put that at risk. Once he has lived with Robert and Jean for a year, he will be theirs. Until then, I have to play everything safe.

That will be six months from now. When the adoption papers are signed, Robert and Jean will be the proud official parents of their son Jeremy. I will not have received a penny from them to bear him.

This doesn't bother me. There are other things that do.

*　　*　　*

When I left Robert's and Jean's house in mid-September, I felt happy and fulfilled, even though the circumstances were so strange. First at the hospital and later at their house, I felt that we had achieved the emotional contact I wanted all along from surrogate motherhood. Some of that warmth and sharing seemed finally to be taking place.

Needless to say, it hadn't always been that way: the three of us had had plenty of ups and downs throughout the pregnancy. But in those final intense days I seemed to have got what I wanted from Robert and Jean. I was proud of doing what I said I'd do, and I felt that we were all bound together by our feelings of love for the baby I'd borne them. I saw how happy Jean had become now she was a mother, and I fully believe that Robert was just as happy in his own way. The surrogacy experience had turned out, or so it seemed, in exactly the way I'd hoped.

I felt that I had particularly grown closer to Jean. Our hours spent caring for the baby, feeding him and changing him, and sitting chatting together in the kitchen, meant a great deal to me. Although nothing was ever said about it, I did feel very strongly that a tie had developed between us, something that would always be there.

Leaving Alan behind had been much easier than I expected. I was relieved to find that I didn't think about him very much: I had feared that I'd suddenly feel his loss almost the way you feel when someone dies. But those feelings didn't develop then, and they still haven't. Over the months I have thought about Alan less and less – only when I see a newborn baby in the street, or in a television advert. Even then, the thought passes quickly, without touching off any raw emotion. I see a baby and think, 'It wasn't so long ago that I had one of those.' But this is mostly because I love little babies.

After leaving Robert and Jean, I had decided not to be the one who initiated contact. I wanted to be tactful: they could ring me if they wanted to, but I would leave it up to them.

After we had been so close for those days together, I more or less assumed that they would.

Robert rang a couple of weeks after I left. He asked how I was, and said that Jean and Jeremy were fine. Jean's mother was staying with them, which was a great help to her, and everything had gone smoothly with the various health visitors who had come round. The health visitor from my GP had been there the day after I left. She saw that everything was fine with the baby, and knew that I had really handed it over to them; presumably she reported back to the GP that everything had gone as planned. I wondered whether she would be impressed that I had gone through with it. Now they were being dealt with by another health visitor, the one from their own GP, with whom the baby had been registered while I was staying there.

I was relieved to hear that all this had worked out as planned. Although I had tried to anticipate every possible complication, it was precisely in dealing with the social services that major problems might have arisen.

Robert did not ring again until early November, almost a month later. His call was mostly just ordinary news. They had told the 'affair' story to the social services, and they appeared to have accepted it. Once Alan had been living with them for over three months, they would officially apply for adoption. This would take some time to finalise, but they had been told that there was no reason to expect any problems.

Robert didn't volunteer much other information, and naturally I was curious about Alan.

'I suppose he's changed a lot,' I said. 'Two months is a long time for a baby. I'll bet I wouldn't recognise him now.' This had been my experience with my second boy: when he was born he was so ugly he looked like a little monkey, but at three months he was as beautiful as could be.

'Oh, I wouldn't say that,' replied Robert. 'He looks pretty much as he did when you last saw him, just a bit fatter.'

'And how's Jean?' I asked. 'Is she coping all right?'

'Yes,' said Robert, 'she's coping just fine.' I waited for elaboration – little stories or something – but none came.

The casual, unforthcoming way in which Robert talked to me was upsetting. Talking to him made me realise how sad I was not to be hearing the news from Jean herself. She hadn't rung me at all, not even to say hello. I had been looking forward to having womanly chats over the telephone, and instead it was like the first weeks of my pregnancy – with Robert acting as a go-between, and Jean and me never talking to each other directly.

In a strange way, that was what I felt: Robert was putting himself between Jean and me. By always being the one who rang (on these and other occasions), he was making it impossible for us to sustain whatever closeness Jean and I had. I now felt that slipping from my grasp – if it had ever been there in the first place. And I was hurt by the thought that Jean had not felt the same strong feeling that I had. Intellectually I could understand that she would not want to maintain the relationship. But perhaps she did still feel it, and was being prevented from continuing with it by Robert. How was I to know?

Despite my sorrow over what had happened between Jean and me, I still felt very strongly that I should leave it up to them to get in touch. I knew that it would be wrong to intrude on their privacy. So I didn't ring them. And the friendly calls I had been expecting did not come.

Robert did ring again, in mid-November, to arrange for the next payment. He said he would drive over to my house the following Saturday. I told him to bring Jean and the baby if he wanted to. I did hope he would, but didn't really expect them to come along. And indeed, he turned up on his own.

Robert was in good spirits, and I enjoyed seeing him. He seemed to be loving the experience of fatherhood, and said that Jean was jokingly hoping I would have another baby for them in due course. I laughed at that along with Robert, but

172

I knew that I would never do it again for someone else. If I had another baby, it would be mine.

With that next payment I had received £5,000, exactly half of the money that was owed to me. The next and final payment fell due in two months.

In the meantime, I didn't hear from Robert and Jean for over a month. I did get a card from them at Christmas time, however. It was signed, 'From Robert and Jean and Jeremy.' I was very pleased and naively hoped that this signalled the beginning of more contact between us all.

* * *

Apart from my disappointment over Robert and Jean, my greatest difficulty during those first months was not having anything on which to focus my strong maternal feelings. Once I left Alan behind I thought I would be able somehow to transfer the feelings onto my own boys. But the boys are too old for that now: they didn't want it. When they suddenly started getting all this attention, they could only assume that Mummy had gone off her rocker.

Even though I had already had two babies, I missed having one now. It wasn't so much Alan as an individual baby that I missed, it was all the things that you do with any baby: caring for it, loving it and playing with it, going down the high street with a pram. Also, when my two were born I didn't have any money, so I couldn't afford all the nice things you like to buy for a baby. (Though really they're not for the baby, they're for yourself. A baby doesn't care whether its cot has a canopy.) And I didn't have the nice home that I have now, a place where I'd really like to have a newborn baby. Also, I felt less confident about children then, so I couldn't enjoy them as much as I would now. I would have more patience, especially when they were young, than I used to. I wouldn't get so upset about the little things they get up to.

When I thought about all the things I missed about not

having a baby at home with me now, I began feeling broody again. This took me by surprise: I hadn't at all intended to have another baby yet. But after leaving Alan behind, I found that my desire for another one was becoming very strong.

This doesn't mean that I wanted Alan back - that I thought about going to Robert's and Jean's house and taking him away from them. I knew I could do that, and so did they. But he wasn't my baby, he was theirs. I wasn't going to try to take him away.

I felt as I had when I was first pregnant with Alan. What I wanted was a baby that was *mine*, mine and John's - conceived by us because we both wanted it. The whole experience would be different. I hadn't fully enjoyed carrying Alan the way I had my own babies: I never felt that I could talk to him in the same way, or play records for him or have little games with him. That would just have made things more difficult. Now I wanted to be able to do that again.

John was sympathetic about these feelings considering that he had not wanted any more children. Now he heard me talking about having another child soon, rather than in five or six years' time as I had sometimes spoken of, and he didn't simply try to talk me out of it. I could see that he still wasn't very keen on it, but he didn't get cross in any way.

Around Christmas time, I noticed a slight change in his attitude. We went into Mothercare to get some clothes as presents for the boys, and instead I went straight to the baby things and started looking at them. I told John what I would buy for a baby if we had another one, and he was actually very interested. We walked around for a while looking at the baby things, and finally he broke off.

'Let's get out of here before I get too excited and we both get carried away.' I realised then that he wouldn't be so opposed to having another baby after all.

'Should we have another one, then?' I asked.

'If that's what you want, we will.'

174

I was so pleased he said that.

For four months or so, I was very keen to get pregnant again. But we did not go out of our way to have intercourse on the right days, and when it didn't happen immediately my strong feelings began to subside, just as they had when I was first pregnant with Alan. Gradually, they more or less disappeared. Not entirely: I still feel that it would be nice, but I'm not going to go out of my way to make it happen. And I managed to channel my intense emotions into my book, which absorbed me more and more.

*　　*　　*

In January, surrogate mothers hit the headlines again, when Kim Cotton gave birth to a baby that she had been paid to have for another couple. She had worked through an American agency and sold her story beforehand to one of the national papers, so it was guaranteed plenty of press coverage. And it was obvious that she hadn't worked out any of the major practical details. When the story was reported, the local council where she had her baby wouldn't let her leave the hospital with it. Such is the price of publicity. I felt sorry for her, and was happy to have avoided those problems myself.

But her problems did indirectly affect me. On the day that her story came out, my agent phoned me to say that the *Observer* was interested in buying the serial rights to my book. And they thought that now would be a good time to break my story. I was ready for this now, as long as all three of us remained anonymous. I certainly didn't want to be exposed as Kim Cotton had. The agents ended up selling serial rights to the *Observer*, which proceeded to run an article about me and what I had done.

Before the article was due to appear, I rang Robert and Jean to tell them about it. I didn't want them to be surprised when they saw it in the newspaper. I assured them that their

175

names would not be published, and that they would not be identifiable through any clues in the article.

I also took this opportunity to tell Robert and Jean of a decision I had made that same day. The *Observer* was going to be paying me money, and I had already signed a contract for my book with a publisher. The sums involved were not a great fortune, but they were plenty for me: and they were all I had ever expected to make from being a surrogate mother. In light of that, I had decided not to demand the rest of the money from Robert and Jean.

I knew that Robert was worried about raising the next instalment; he had mentioned this on one of the few occasions when he rang. Feeling quite excited by the fact that my story was being told – and that extra money was coming in – I felt a rush of generosity.

When I got through to Robert, I told him about the book and the article. Because of them, I said that I was quite happy with the amount I had already received from him, and that we could call it quits.

Robert actually seemed surprised that my book had got so far. But most of all, he was tremendously relieved about the money.

'That's great,' he said. 'I feel much better now that the debt to you is out of the way. I'm very grateful.' Then he added, as if in afterthought, 'Now I feel as if I've had my fair share of your book.'

I was shocked by that. He clearly felt that he was entitled to some of the proceeds of the book, that a cut was due to him. It satisfied him to think that I wasn't making *all* the money from it. Whatever qualms I might have felt about writing it, his reaction made them disappear.

If I was expecting a more wholehearted expression of gratitude, I was to be disappointed.

So that was it. They had paid me £5,000 in all. They owed me nothing more. All I had to do was sign the adoption papers when the time came. Thinking back on it now, I realise that calling it quits over money was my way of saying that their friendship meant more to me than the cash. That was what I wanted from them most of all. I hoped they would recognise this. If they had, they didn't let on about it.

*　　*　　*

At home, my friends and neighbours had all been very kind and sympathetic about the 'tragedy'. They had come over with flowers and offered their condolences, and they really were good-hearted about it. After the first few days they tactfully never brought up the subject again, and it seemed to have been forgotten. People got on with their lives. It was just as I had hoped.

But it was difficult keeping up my lies in the face of their sympathy. I felt very uncomfortable about that. Still, I was surprised by the ease with which I managed to lie to them and keep up all the pretences.

My boys, thankfully, seemed to forget very quickly about the baby brother they had never seen. Now they don't ask about him at all.

With my mother-in-law, matters did not turn out as I expected. My conscience got the better of me. Betty had been very kind and concerned about the so-called death of my baby, but I could tell that she was also upset about the death of her grandchild. I hated pretending with her, and the idea of keeping up the lie for the rest of my life became increasingly intolerable. After about five months, I finally knew that I had to confess and tell her the truth.

I did it one day in February, when she and Jack were in town to stay with us. John was still out at work and Jack had taken the boys to the park. Betty and I were doing a bit of spring-cleaning in the kitchen. We had been chatting about this and that, and I decided the time was now or never. I took a deep breath.

'Betty, there's something I've got to tell you about. I don't

177

know how you're going to feel about this, but . . .' It was hard to keep talking, my heart was racing so fast. I really didn't have any idea how she would react.

'Betty, my baby didn't die.'

Her eyes opened wide, her jaw dropped; she sat down heavily in a chair. One thing was obvious: she had never suspected a thing till now.

When I had given her a moment to recover, I told her the whole story. Betty listened in silence, and when I'd finished, she wasn't smiling. But she didn't look angry, either. There was a long silence.

'Well,' she said finally, 'I'm very very glad the baby didn't die after all.' She spoke in a soft voice. I could tell that she was having a hard time taking in what I'd told her, but I certainly felt much better for having got it off my chest. I gave her the article from the *Observer* and waited for her to read it. When she had finished, she handed it back, and then she kissed me on the forehead.

'It's very interesting,' she said. 'I don't know *why* you did it, and I don't know *how* you did it, but I still love you, and your secret stays safe with me.'

She asked me quite a lot of questions but I could tell she didn't want to push me. I told her the whole truth. Afterwards I hugged her. How lucky I was to have such a good mother-in-law, I thought to myself! John had said right from the start that she would be broad-minded about this, and he had been proved right. Since then, Betty has not mentioned the subject, though she did say she would like to read my book when it was finished.

*　　*　　*

It was in March that my solicitor rang up to say that he thought I should hand back the money to Robert and Jean. I agreed with him immediately once he had explained the situation. By now, so many months had passed that I

178

knew there was no hope of things getting warmer and friendlier between the three of us. They had made their desires clear. They did not want contact with me. That hurt me deeply.

But whatever feelings I had about them, I would never have done anything to put Alan's future at risk. And with money coming in from the book and newspaper article, I would be able to pay the money back fairly easily.

I hadn't spoken to Robert since just before the newspaper article appeared in January. I phoned him after speaking to my solicitor and told him that I was returning the money in a post-dated cheque. When I had cash in my account, the money would be theirs.

Naturally he was delighted, as I would have expected. But I would also have expected something more. If I had been in his position, I'd have felt a little shifty at getting away without paying anything. I'd have said that I was sorry for the sake of the person giving the money back, and insisted that some other gesture, a token of goodwill, be made. Robert didn't say anything like this. He simply said he was glad to be getting the money back; he and Jean could use it at the moment.

We did chat a little. Robert said that the baby was very well, and that Jean was very happy. Her mother was gone, and Jean was settling into motherhood on her own very nicely. He also said that they had applied to adopt the baby, though this would take another nine months before it could be finalised.

I acted cheerful while talking to him, but this conversation left a bitter taste in my mouth. I realised that I had not spoken to Jean since the day I left their house – nearly six months before. She had not phoned me once. I had long since accepted that we were not going to be the best of pals forever, but I thought that some of the closeness we had touched on during my stay would remain. Now I had to conclude that I had been completely wrong. Jean considered me gone from her life. What I had done did not mean to her anything like what it had meant to me. And Robert's reaction to my news about the cheque suggested that, for him, the arrangement was very simple: I was having a baby for money, and now I had got it from the book. That the money wasn't his didn't matter to him. He seemed to have no inkling of the sacrifice I had made for them, or of the fact that what I had done might in some sense be a personal gesture towards him and Jean. Now they had no reason for getting in touch with me until the adoption papers needed signing.

I felt totally empty. For the first time I started thinking that Robert and Jean had used me. That feeling has persisted.

*   *   *

Months of silence have followed that brief conversation with Robert. John remarked the other day that they would like to forget that I ever existed. Now I'm inclined to agree with him. On my last day at their house, I had clearly been delighted when they offered to send me a picture of Alan. The photograph never came. I have nothing to remind me of him.

If I could go back to the beginning, what would I – what *could* I – do differently? I would still be willing to act as a surrogate mother, but I suppose that I might have tried to find a different couple to have a baby for. I had hoped at the beginning to spend much more time with the couple than I ended up spending with Robert and Jean. I thought we might go out on picnics together during the summer, or that I might spend the odd weekend at their house, or go shopping more with Jean – anything that would enable me to get to know them better in a friendly, informal environment. Going out to restaurants with them gave me very little idea of what they were really like.

Obviously they wanted it this way: they are very private

people. I now see that I hardly learnt anything about them. I didn't even get much insight into their home life during the time that I did stay with them.

It was naive of me to expect anything different, and probably that was my big mistake. I expected too much from the relationship. But I don't believe that justifies their behaviour. I gave them so much, yet in the end they denied me not only their friendship but the courtesy you might expect of any casual acquaintance. Failing to send the promised photograph was only the final act of carelessness. People talk of babies who are rejected. In this case, it is the mother who has been rejected.

I remind myself constantly that feelings other than mine must be taken into account. Robert and Jean believe that it is better not to have any more contact, and for all I know they are right. Yet they never had the courtesy to say so openly. They knew that this was what I wanted, and they should have told me that they weren't prepared to give it. They certainly got what they wanted from me.

In a way, writing this book has provided the only outlet for all the feelings that went unsatisfied. Putting my sadness down in words has relieved it, if only a little bit.

* * *

I don't think Robert and Jean would object to my seeing the baby, but they must feel that the more I'm around the harder it will be to forget where their baby came from. Even though they don't feel any shame about it, I don't think they feel that my presence will help them see Alan as truly their own.

I would like to see Alan, though still out of curiosity only. At one time I was afraid of seeing him too soon: I thought he might recognise me, and I would hate to do anything to upset him. I'm sure that now, many months after he was separated from me, there is no danger of that. But the option of seeing him has not been offered to me.

It's been so many months now that I hardly remember what he looks like. I think that only instinct would tell me that he was a baby I had given birth to.

On the few occasions when I do think about him, a strange feeling comes over me. I wonder whose baby he really was: was he mine or not? I can't answer that question now, and I don't think I will ever be able to.

But however sad I feel, I don't regret what I did. And I'm glad to have the opportunity to tell my story – to show how one woman can help another by giving her what she wants more than anything in the world. You can be sure that, whatever has happened between his parents and me, the baby I gave to Robert and Jean will be one of the most wanted and best loved babies in Britain.